First published 2014 by Fusion Retro Books
Fusion Retro Books, 51 Dencer Drive, Kenilworth, CV8 2QR
http://www.fusionretrobooks.com

Printed and bound by **mcc**graphics

Acknowledgements

- ■ ❏ ■ **Sir Clive Sinclair** for inventing a machine that has meant so much to so many for so long. Without the Sinclair ZX Spectrum I would not be in the industry I am in today, and this book would not exist!
- ■ ❏ ■ **Mark R. Jones** for supplying a great deal of the visual content and helping with the proof-reading of this book. You are a star as always.
- ■ ❏ ■ **Rick Dickinson** for designing a British icon and giving up his time to talk 'Sinclair'.
- ■ ❏ ■ **Spanner Spencer & Dan Whitehead** for being the awesome writers they are and contributing to the game reviews. **Gareth Perch** for proof reading.
- ■ ❏ ■ **Martyn Carroll** for writing his ZX Spectrum story for the book. You pulled me back in retro gaming when you launched Retro Gamer back in the day - thanks mate, you will always be my hero.
- ■ ❏ ■ **Roger Kean** for being a professional, a gentleman and the individual who gave us *Crash*, *Zzap 64!* and *Amtix!* magazines.
- ■ ❏ ■ **Oliver Frey** for the kind permission to use his artwork, and for also giving us *Crash*, *Zzap 64!* and *Amtix!* magazines.
- ■ ❏ ■ **Steven Day** for creating an iconic cover.
- ■ ❏ ■ **Tim @ Rockrabillia** for supplying the mint 128K Spectrum pictures.
- ■ ❏ ■ **And the family** – my wife Nomita, daughters Amber and Sienna and son Milan, who once again gave me the time I needed alone in my man-cave to put this book together. Love you guys as always.

CONTENTS

foreword

By living in a coastal town in South West Wales I was exposed to the arcades at the local seaside resorts. These colourful, loud and brash places were home to all the lastest gaming machines and once discovered, I just couldn't keep away. I remember cycling the four or so miles down to the nearest one each day of the school summer holidays, dumping the bike and running into one of the two arcades on the sea front. I had no money to play the games - I was just happy to watch others hone their skills.

On returning to school after the break, excitement was brewing in the playground in regards to the successor of the ZX81 called the ZX Spectrum. Clive Sinclair's new computer was going to sport seven colours and be able to produce sound for the first time. Owning a ZX Spectrum would mean, in theory, I would be able to play all the games I had seen in the summer in the comfort of my own bedroom and without the need of a bottomless pit of 10p coins.

I literally begged my parents for a computer that year for Christmas using all the excuses under the sun why I needed one - I made it quite clear the 48K version of the Spectrum was the one Santa should bring.

My parents are the best - on Christmas morning I received a shiny new boxed 48K Spectrum with two games - *Lunar Jetman* by Ultimate Play the Game and *Manic Miner* by Bug-Byte Software. Christmas 1983, at the tender age of 13, was my best childhood Christmas by far.

Over the coming months my gaming collection grew and the following long winter evenings were spent furthering hi-scores on my favourite titles.

For Christmas 1984 my main present was the ZX Expansion Set. With the Multiface One I could now copy games onto cartridge via the ZX Microdrive and load them in a fraction of the time it took from tape.

Further peripherals that I magically acquired included a Kempston Interface, Quickshot 1 joystick, µCurrah Speech Synthesiser, Dk'Tronics keyboard and an AMX mouse.

The local newsagent used to push Crash magazine through the letterbox each month. Each Saturday morning, when the family did the weekly shop, I caught up with more news and reviews in all the other Spectrum gaming magazines at WH Smiths to get comparitive scores for the upcoming games.

I spent my hard earned pocket money on games when I could afford to - it was in the playground though where my collection grew - swapping C15 tapes full of copied games with my friends.

Move forward a couple of years, and after learning BASIC by typing in many a game listing from the various magazines that hosted them, I purchased a copy of YS MegaBASIC from Your Sinclair magazine. It was written by Mike Leaman and allowed extended functions in BASIC and meant I could type 'properly' on my Dk'Tronics keyboard as opposed to Symbol Shift this and Extended Shift that. I wrote my O Level Computer Studies project using that application - an accounts package to keep track of incoming and outgoing transactions. I printed out the program on my Alphacom 32 printer and still have a copy, albeit very faded, of the listing to this day. I got an 'A' grade at O Level with the help of my Spectrum and to celebrate, I exchanged it for a Sinclair +2 pack that included some Ocean games.

Having only experienced the simple sound effects that the 48K Spectrum could produce, up until that time, hearing Jonathan Dunn's *Robocop* tune coming through the speaker of my TV was a 'moment' for me. Every game I purchased for a while from then had to be the more expensive 128K version that sported a great soundtrack - *Starglider*, *Hydrofool*, *Amaurote*, *Three Weeks in Paradise*, *Thundercats*, *Glider Rider*, *Target: Renegade* (the list goes on).

Even to this day I am still an avid ZX Spectrum fan and have regularly played the games over the years using emulation and, now and again, at the many retro gaming events that have become popular.

It's been great putting this book together and having the opportunity to talk to some of those who made the games I played some 30 plus years ago. Meeting up with Rick Dickinson, the very person who designed many of Sinclair's products including the ZX Spectrum, was another special moment for me. I was given an oppurtunity to thank him for creating something that has been cherished by so many for so long and an item that also jump-started my career in IT.

I hope you enjoy the book and get as nostalgic and gooey eyed as I do, when I look back at the games - the games we played back at an innocent part of our lives, when anything was possible and where, by typing a few commands into the Spectrum, the TV could be made to do more things than show Blue Peter or the latest episode of Top of the Pops.

Time to go - I need to have another go of *Jetpac* before bed. I have a hi-score to beat you know.

Rick Dickinson

The designer of the Sinclair ZX80, ZX81, 16K/48K Spectrum, Spectrum + and Spectrum 128K computers.

I studied a sandwich placement course on 'Design For Industry' at Newcastle. My first three-month placement was a disaster and when the second placement came around in the third year I was far more careful and selective on the placement I chose. I was offered an interview with John Pemberton of Sinclair Radionics – these guys had produced some great tech and being such a fan I had pictures of all their products in my scrapbook. I had an interview and got a three-month placement with them. At the end of the stint I did not want to leave – I was good though and went back and did my final year and ultimately graduated with a 1st Class Honours.

After graduation in 1979, I had no idea what I wanted to do – I stayed with my parents in Mumbles in South Wales, and applied for no end of jobs. In the meantime to raise some living money I applied for some odd jobs including ones for a gravedigger and a taxi driver. I never got the jobs, being told I was overqualified.

Out of the blue, a telegram came through from John Pemberton saying 'Ring me, ASAP'. So I did. He said he was leaving Sinclair and wanted me to come and apply for his position at the company. I went for an interview with Clive Sinclair, and was given the job.

I was apprehensive. John had won awards all over and had a huge amount of experience and I had no idea of how I would fill his shoes. If my situation was a design on the drawing board it would be in the bin by now. There was an overlap of working with John (of three months or so) before he left. He said, 'Look it is common sense and the bits you don't know, well you just bluff your way through

Rick chilling in between designs.

that'. And he was right. I finished off the design of the ZX80 and for each decision that was to be made I imagined what John's solution would have been. With the ZX80 the assumption was that it would sell to the hobbyist market – Clive was familiar with this market and a target shipment per month was set. The reality was there were sacks and sacks of cheques from those who wanted the ZX80 – it was actually difficult to get into the office each day due to the bags of money everywhere.

Clive promised me there would be a new product soon, and there was.

He called me into his room for a briefing and from that meeting I went away with his vision of the successor to the ZX80, the ZX81 - it was little more than an evolved version of the ZX80. I went on to design that computer for Sinclair and it won the company an award - a 'British Design Council Award'.

The Spectrum was the Next Big Thing for Sinclair and it was a huge turning point for the company. Two big design decisions happened – going from monochrome to colour and the provision of a tactile keyboard.

There was a lot of criticism directed towards the ZX80 and ZX81's keyboard – the consumer sometimes forgets there is always a reason for a design decision. In this case compromises were made to ensure the computer could be sold for less than £100. The Spectrum had a 'moving key' keyboard with the keys made out of silicon rubber and actuated on a keyboard underneath using similar technology to

that found in the ZX81. My job was to make the Spectrum, with its new keyboard, as small and elegant as possible and as some of the design sketches show, it was difficult to get all the information on the keys that those writing the software needed. Decisions had to be made on what bits of information went on the top and bottom of the key - would owners mix up the info on the row below with the keys above?

The design room where many of Sinclair's famous products were designed by Rick.

"The Spectrum was the Next Big Thing for Sinclair and it was a huge turning point for the company."

A Spectrum + painted white.

The smallest that a key could be was determined by the lettering of the largest BASIC command needing printing on the key.

When the size of each key was agreed and all the keys were in place and where they should be on the keyboard, well this would be the width of the ZX Spectrum.

The thickness of the computer was set by the height of the TV modulator - this gave a space to the right where the heat sink could be housed. We had no idea really how hot the Spectrum would get – we bolted the heat sink onto the PCB, made it as big as we could and hoped it would do the job.

Placing the space bar in the traditional location would make the Spectrum bigger than it needed to be - Clive was adamant that every micron counted so it was decided to sneak it into the bottom right corner.

"Placing the space bar in the traditional location would make the Spectrum bigger than it needed to be ."

During the design stage I would make sketches and show Clive – he knew what he wanted and we would agree if it worked or not. It would then take a few weeks for me to actually make a model out of acrylic sheet by hand – a solid block that would be carved away until the design of the computer came through. The keys on the model were made out of cardboard and the lettering added painstakingly by pen. The production drawings for each part of the

computer would then be made.

We had to decide what materials to use on the Spectrum. Injection moulding struggles with holes so the keyboard would pose a problem. We therefore built the Spectrum keyboard plate using aluminium and found a company in West Bromwich (Thomas Cook and Son) that could do the holes, bend the aluminium and print litho lettering onto it with a perfect finish each time. It was important that all the bits of the Spectrum came together in the design process to form a perfect fit – this meant spending a lot of time

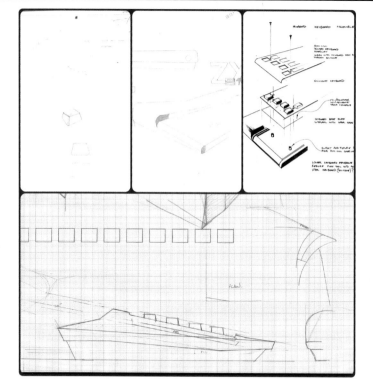

Original design sketches of the ZX Spectrum.

with the manufacturer. I remember going to Thomas Cook for the first time and placing the plate onto the injection plastic moulding case and it fitted perfectly. That was a great moment.

The initial Spectrum had grey keys, Clive thought that the computer needed more colour so blue keys were introduced – when Clive made a decision it happened.

The reset button and on/off switch were discussed as part of the design - Clive always questioned why they were needed. His argument was that when you flicked the power on, just seeing the screen with the Sinclair logo meant the computer was on – who needed an LED? To reset the computer just meant switching it off and on again at the wall.

When we designed the Spectrum we had no peripherals so we made a provision for future expansion by providing a basic edge connector for devices to connect. The design was not perfect as the connector could, being made out of tin, oxidise. Many of the peripherals made for the Spectrum had gold connectors – this proved fruitless though as connecting with the tin connector of the Spectrum could give variable results due to poor connection.

The Interface 1 was the only extension that was secured to the Spectrum via screws, thus at least stopping the 'wobble' effect that could interrupt the connection with the connector.

The QL was launched before the Spectrum + and with marketing promoting the machine for business use it had to have a proper moving keyboard. As we had spent so much money on the keyboard, including moulded lettering, it made sense to use it on the Spectrum +. With Clive softening at this time he started to say yes to a number of things that the consumer was asking for, like a reset button, a full space bar and the legs at the bottom to raise the angle of typing.

> ## *"The reset button and on / off switch were discussed as part of the design."*

It was a rush to get the Spectrum + out, thus the corporate style of the QL was copied over to the design. The inside was just a normal Spectrum PCB with a reset button wired in. Without doubt, much more love and passion was put into the Spectrum 16K/48K than the + which was just a turnkey product.

"It was all about getting something to market quickly so we re-used the + case and stuck an external heat sink on the outside of the computer."

The keyboard for the QL used much more of an architectural approach in its design to make it look as different as it could to any other keyboards out there. Quality at the time was questionable and keys could drop out.

The key tops were moulded and created in Sweden and the plunger moulding was tooled in a factory in Italy by a husband/wife team. We had a plane in those days, so I flew over with David Chatten, the Operations Controller, to the factory to see the first plungers off the assembly line for the QL. The keyboard key is a push fit onto the plunger and is held on by a friction fit and it was expected that the fit would not be perfect first time resulting in a process of refining until it fitted correctly. We put all the keys into our model, turned the QL upside down and five or so fell out. I shook it and five more fell out. Dave asked how long it would take to tweak the design and they replied three weeks. We didn't have that kind of time so David just told them to run the production. Reports

started to appear in the press where early adopters of the QL and Spectrum + were experiencing a few problems with their keyboards.

The 128K was a completely different machine, though looking very similar to the +. Sinclair had to pander to the gaming market and give the gamers some of the things they were asking for – more memory and three channel sound for example.

It was all about getting something to market quickly so we re-used the + case and stuck an external heat sink on the outside of the computer to help with the heat created by the extra tech inside the box.

The 128K had many ports that went

The Spectrum 128K showing off its numeric keypad.

against the minimalist design of previous computers – with Clive having very little input to the Spectrum at this stage, we put whatever was available in the machine. The numeric pad was a day's work of design – we used the same keys and made the design the same as the 128K. I did not even create a model for it.

I left Sinclair before its journey was finished. The company went through a very unhappy phase, which ultimately ended in its demise and Sugar buying it. I remember asking Clive if we could meet and he agreed. After we got together Clive got straight to the point and asked what was on my mind and I remember telling him I did not like the company any more. And Clive replied, 'Neither do I!'

A new ZX Spectrum? Design prototypes created by Rick, October 2014.

At the time there were suspicions that there was a mole from Amstrad in marketing and everything we did was getting back to Alan Sugar. If the rumours were true, Sugar had all of our products stuck to a wall in a meeting room and he met with his aides regularly to discuss Sinclair and how he could accelerate our demise. Having him take over was like putting the wolf in amongst the sheep.

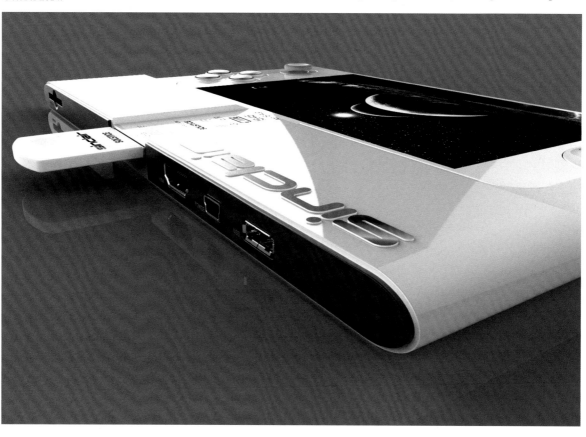

SPREAD THE WORD.

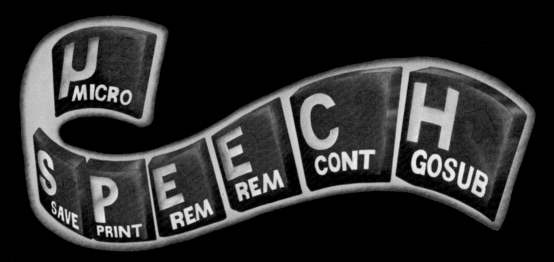

EXPERIENCE THE DEVASTATING SOUND OF MICROSPEECH ON YOUR SPECTRUM

μ EVERYONE FINDS IT FUN BECAUSE IT'S EASY TO USE
(it says any word you want it to say)

μ EXCLUSIVE TECHNOLOGY MEANS ALL SOUND IS NOW PUT THROUGH YOUR TV

μ AND THE GAMES WITH SPEECH............ SPEAK FOR THEMSELVES

.................ULTIMATE..Lunar Jetman......BUG BYTE..Birds and the Bees......OCEAN..Mr Wimpy..Hunchback..Moon Alert......QUICKSILVA..Mined Out......................
............ROMIK..3D Monster Chase..Shark Attack..Colour Clash......MARTECH..Blastermind......MOGUL..Las Vegas Lady....CRYSTAL..The Island.............
..........DIGITAL FANTASIA..Mysterious Adventures (Parts 1-10)......LYVERSOFT..Lunar Rescue......BRITANNIA..Grand Prix Driver......CDS.. Time Bomb................
.............ARCADIA..Mushroom Mania......PSS..Blade Alley......MR MICRO..Crazy Golf..Punchy..Harlequin......DkTRONICS..Maziacs.................

(some of these games are new versions of original programs)

AND THIS ISN'T THE END OF IT!

NEW PROGRAMS FROM

POSTERN
VIRGIN
SALAMANDER
VISIONS
INCENTIVE
MIKROGEN
SOFTEK
ABBEX
ANIROG
AUTOMATA
HEWSON CONSULTANTS
RICHARD SHEPHERD
SOFTWARE PROJECTS
THOR
FANTASY
MICROMANIA
M.C.LOTHLORIEN

WILL BE APPEARING SOON

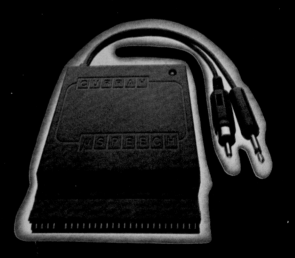

AVAILABLE FROM COMPUTER DEALERS NATIONWIDE INCLUDING

COMET . W. H. SMITH . JOHN MENZIES . WOOLWORTHS . GREENS . SPECTRUM

COMPLETE DETAILS ARE ON OUR LEAFLET

PICK ONE UP FROM ANY STORE

CURRAH
μSPEECH   ONLY **£29.95** EACH

including   μ FREE SPEECH GAME "MYSTIC TOWER"

μ COMPREHENSIVE MANUAL

μ DEMO CASSETTE

Martyn Carroll

Lifelong Spectrum fan and original Retro Gamer editor Martyn Carroll paints a picture of his youth in hues of red, yellow, green and cyan.

Look back at the ZX Spectrum and you think about colour clash, beeping sound, rubber keys and R Tape Loading Error and you wonder if the primitive thing deserves to be revered in memory at all; but then you remember dabbling in BASIC and Crash magazine and 'Hey Hey 16K' and games. Always the games. *Ant Attack*, *Manic Miner*, *Turbo Esprit* and *Head over Heels*. Just four great games from a thousand and more that were developed for – and defined – the Spectrum.

The first game I ever played on the Spectrum was far from great, but for a saucer-eyed seven-year-old it was frankly amazing. The game was *Muncher!*, a *Pacman* clone from Silversoft. My father brought it home for our new Spectrum (I say 'our', but the computer was actually bought for my brother, who was six years older than me and far more persuasive in his pestering). Now our dad wasn't daft. He wasn't buying the 'help with homework' line. Nor did he have any hair-brained plans to compute the household accounts. He knew we wanted it for games. He'd seen the pair of us in his office at work, completely wired, playing games on a massive Commodore PET that hogged half the desk.

I'm not exactly sure why he chose the Spectrum and not one of the many other home computers that flooded onto the market in the early 80s. A VIC-20 would have been a more obvious choice, particularly as he used a Commodore computer at work. I presume my brother pushed the Spectrum as some of his friends already owned one. I also believe my dad was attached to the Sinclair name. He'd witnessed the rise of Clive Sinclair and his establishment as Britain's foremost boffin.

Muncher! by Silversoft, released in 1982.

My dad was in manufacturing so buying British was important to him. It must have been – he drove a Morris Marina after all.

The fact that it was cheap was also a factor. It was a plaything after all, so he wasn't about to stump up hundreds of pounds so we could chomp fruit and chase ghosts. The 16K Spectrum launched in 1982 at £125 and in 1983 dropped to £99, making it the first colour computer that you could buy in the UK for less than £99. That was the price breakthrough that convinced my dad and no doubt many others. But it was still no impulse purchase. Factor in inflation and that £99 was more like £300 in today's money. In 2014, the cheaper Spectrum would cost the same as an Xbox One or PlayStation 4.

So a 16K Spectrum was acquired and much *Muncher!* was played. Shortly after, one game became two as a *Space Invaders* clone called *Spectral Invaders* was added. I'd previously stood on tip-toes, watching my brother play coin-ops in seaside arcades, and now we had versions of these classic games in our own home. It was bliss. Over the months the game collection slowly grew. *Jetpac* and the other early titles from Ultimate Play the Game were obvious highlights – even in my short trousers I could see they were a clear cut above. A Kempston interface and Competition Pro joystick were added for that proper

The Competition Pro joystick - the controller of choice for the Spectrum gamer.

arcade-at-home feel. I remember my brother writing off to the various software houses and receiving lovely A2 game posters in return. He wasn't the only one. The Stampers, the brothers behind Ultimate, later revealed that they had to employ someone full time just to deal with the amount of fan mail for fear of being buried beneath it.

These were good times, no doubt, and

Christmas 1986 in the Carroll house. Martyn proudly pictured with *They Sold a Million 3*. On the floor are copies of *Their Finest Hour*, *The Lord of the Rings* and *Dynamite Dan II*.

ZX SPECTRUM 16K / 48K

ZX Spectrum 16K / 48K

The ZX Spectrum was launched in 1982 and was based on the Zilog Z80 processor. The original model had 16KB of Random Access Memory and retailed for £125 - 48KB models soon followed for a whopping £175. The Spectrum sported a distinct rubber keyed keyboard with a large expansion bay for connecting popular peripherals like the ZX Printer and Interface 1 / ZX Microdrive.

they were about to get even better.

Fast forward to 1985 and the Spectrum had become massively popular. It was the best-selling computer in the UK, occupying more than 40% of the market and leading a largely three horse race with the Commodore 64 and Amstrad CPC trailing behind and many of the other runners fallen. Sinclair was experiencing success overseas too, particularly in Europe. The firm also released an updated model, the Spectrum +, which featured new casing and an improved plastic keyboard.

A small selection of Martyn's tape games, including that original copy of Silversoft's *Muncher*!

> ### *"There were hardly any 16K games available, at least relative to the flourishing 48K catalogue, and I already owned most of the best titles."*

In the Carroll household the only change was that the Spectrum now belonged to me. My brother had moved on from playing games and those Ultimate and Imagine posters in his bedroom had been replaced by posters of The Cure and Kate Bush.

The Spectrum was moved into my room and hooked up to a small portable television. There was just one problem – memory. 16K was fine for simple arcade games but for bigger, more ambitious games you needed 48K. Plus, there were hardly any 16K games available, at least relative to the flourishing 48K catalogue, and I already owned most of the best titles: Ultimate's first four titles, the Horace games, *Jumping Jack*, *Styx* and of course *Deathchase*. I'd go into computer shops and there would be just the odd 16K game peeking out from behind stacks of 48K titles. We owned a Betamax VCR (you'll be unsurprised to hear), so it was the same as going into a video hire shop and being faced with a wall of VHS. To compound matters, many of my school friends had 48K models and they'd chat about games I couldn't play. I'd also started getting Sinclair User magazine on a regular basis so I could read about these unattainable titles as well as hear about them. My Spectrum was vanilla and I wanted neapolitan.

After much pleading my dad finally

conceded and bought me
a Spectrum+ for my 10th
birthday. Finally I could tap that
massive library of 48K software.
My main memory of that
time is not unboxing the new
computer and carefully setting
it up, but rather rushing into
town and spending my birthday
money on two titles – *Jack the
Nipper* (partly because it looked

like fun, partly because it came
with a free badge) and *They Sold a Million*,
the compilation that featured *Sabre Wulf*,
Jet Set Willy, *Daley Thompson's Decathlon*
and *Beach-Head*. Those five games kept
me occupied for months (and at least one
joystick was sacrificed at the altar of *Daley*).
It was *Jet Set Willy* that made the biggest
impression. To me it was like being given
the keys to a real 60-room mansion and
being urged to explore. I always thought
of it as more of an adventure game than a
platformer and I was happy to get lost in
Willy's house for hours.

The period between 1984 and 1986 was
surely the golden age of Spectrum gaming.

The number of truly great games released
was almost embarrassing. Platformers like
Monty Mole and *Dynamite Dan*, isometric
adventures like *Knight Lore* and *Fairlight*,
action games like *Saboteur* and *Quazatron*,
strategy titles like *Chaos* and *Rebelstar*.
And then there are those unique titles that
you can't easily pigeon-hole, such as *Skool
Daze*, *Highway Encounter*, *Thanatos* and
The Lords of Midnight. There was a lot of
originality on display, largely because the
licensed titles and coin-op conversions
had yet to really take hold. But if you
wanted licences then *Trap Door*, *Dan Dare*,
Cobra and *Batman* (the 3D one) were all
excellent. Some of the arcade conversions
from this period were surprisingly
faithful too, such as *Bomb Jack*,
Commando, *Green Beret* and *Space
Harrier*.

This rich software library
showcased the Spectrum as a
capable little computer. It may
have lacked features that other
8-bits boasted, stuff like hardware
sprites, multiple video modes
and dedicated audio chips, but it

ZX SPECTRUM +

ZX Spectrum +

The ZX Spectrum + tried to address the huge bug-bear of the original 48K model, the keyboard. One could argue that the + keyboard should have been a lot better than it was - reports soon came in after launch that keys were falling out of the machine if held upside down. One other bonus that made the upgrade somewhat worthwhile was a reset button.

ZX SPECTRUM 128K

ZX Spectrum 128K

The ZX Spectrum 128K was the last Spectrum released by Sinclair and sported 128K of memory and a 3-channel AY sound chip. The appearance of the machine was the same as the + with the exception of a large heatsink on the right end of the case. At the back are a few new ports - MIDI port, RS-232 serial port and an RGB monitor port. The 128K had no internal speaker like its predecessors with sound coming out of the TV instead.

was still able to compete favourably with its more expensive rivals. I certainly wasn't blinkered by the Spectrum as several of my friends owned other computers and I'd regularly play on Commodore, Amstrad and Acorn machines. Indeed my very best friend who lived three doors up was a Commodore 64 kid and we'd eagerly compare the same big name games on our systems. Sometimes the Spectrum version would be better, sometimes the C64 would win out. It was never one-sided. It should also be noted that the Spectrum was home to authentic versions of games made famous on other machines like *Elite*, *The Way of the Exploding Fist*, *Uridium* and *Starglider*.

The Spectrum version of 16-bit hit *Starglider* was an extraordinary achievement, but it left a bitter aftertaste in my mouth.

"So I obsessed and pressed and eventually convinced my dad into buying a +3 which I received in 1989."

This was the first game of note that was developed specifically for Sinclair's new 128K Spectrum – the 48K version was missing several key features. I'd only had my 48K machine for a few months and yet here I was, hankering after the 'next' Spectrum with its bigger memory and better sound (thanks to a dedicated AY audio chip). The improved BASIC

editor was also a draw as I'd been dabbling in game creation (I managed to get one of my primitive efforts featured in Sinclair User's 'Worst Games' competition, to my immense delight).

I now know that most of the very best Spectrum games run just fine on a modest 48K model, but at the time it was gutting to see 128K versions of games featuring AY sound and no multi-load. I made do with my Spectrum + and merely admired the Spectrum +2 model which Amstrad released following the Sinclair buyout in early 1986.

That machine featured an integrated tape deck, but the subsequent model, the +3 with its built-in disk drive, was far harder to ignore. It's easy to get nostalgic about tapes and reminisce about eating your tea or watching Danger Mouse while games loaded, but let's be honest – tapes were painfully slow and prone to failure.

There were alternatives to tapes of course, notably Sinclair's own Microdrive and Interface 2 add-ons (I loved the idea

They Sold a Million, itself selling over a million copies, provided months of entertainment.

Lotus Esprit Challenge on the ZX Spectrum - more Lada than Lotus.

Romantic Robot's Multiface 3 - the definitive companion to the Spectrum +3.

time going through my existing games and discovering the 128K extras – the bonus stage in *Renegade*, the speech in *Starglider*, the music in *Out Run*. It was amazing to hear Spectrum sound blasting out of the TV rather than being emitted from the computer's innards. I picked up *Robocop* and *Chase HQ* – both on disk – and played them to death. But if I'm honest I bought many more games on tape than disk, simply because they were cheaper. The following year I received a Multiface 3, that wonderful box of tricks from Romantic Robot, and used it to transfer tape games to disk for speedy loading. The +3 and Multiface 3 was an unbeatable combo.

I hadn't realised until just now that our house had been running a tight three-year refresh cycle, with three Spectrum models purchased over the course of nine years. Following the pattern, I upgraded to a new computer in 1992 – but it was no Spectrum. If there had been a new, more capable Spectrum model that still supported my vast library of games then I would have certainly considered it. The closest thing to that was the SAM Coupe and look what happened there. By the time you'd bought a SAM and added a disk drive and mouse the outlay wasn't far off a 16-bit Atari ST or Amiga 500 package. It was the Amiga I went with. I remember going to a friend's house and witnessing *Lotus Esprit Turbo*

of the latter but already owned most of the cartridge games on cassette). I knew about the third-party disk options too but they were expensive and a bit baffling. The +3 brought official disk support to the Spectrum and publishers started to release their wares on 3-inch floppies. I obsessed about the +3. My Spectrum was neapolitan and I wanted double choc and sprinkles.

So I obsessed and pressed and eventually convinced my dad into buying a +3 which I received in 1989. I spent a lot of

ZX SPECTRUM +2 / +2A/B

ZX Spectrum +2/+2A/+2B

The ZX Spectrum +2 was Amstrad's first Spectrum and featured a grey case with spring loaded keys, two joystick ports and a built in cassette player named the 'Datacorder'. The ZX Spectrum +2A is a variant of the +3 and the board inside would behave accordingly if a cassette player was attached or a floppy disk controller - cosmetically it looked like the +2 but sported a black case. A revision of the +2 was made, called the +2B, that featured a dedicated motherboard and enhancements to the audio output.

ZX SPECTRUM +3 / +3B

ZX Spectrum +3

The +3 looked the same as the +2B but featured a built-in 3-inch floppy disk drive instead of a tape drive. Core changes to the hardware caused incompatibilities with older 48K and 128K games. The Interface 1 and Microdrive were also not compatible due to differences in the expansion adaptor. A revision of the +3 was made, called the +3B, that featured a dedicated motherboard and enhancements to the audio output.

Challenge on his Amiga and then rushing out to get the Spectrum version. It was perfectly fine but compared to the Amiga version it was more Lada than Lotus. My mind was made up and the Spectrum was soon consigned to the loft.

I loved the Amiga and lapped up its games, although I was now at college and into other things so I don't remember that period with the same clarity as the Spectrum days. I do recall flicking through a friend's box of Amiga disks sometime around 1996 and finding one with the word 'Speccy' scrawled on the label. The disk contained a Spectrum emulator for the Amiga and ten or so games.

At the time I had no idea about emulation, so this was momentous! The Amiga struggled to run the games at full speed but it didn't matter – I was playing *Jet Set Willy* again, revisiting Willy's abode after a decade away.

"I was playing Jet Set Willy again, revisiting Willy's abode after a decade away."

What was wide-eyed awe then was pure nostalgia now. It was comforting. It was compulsive. Under emulation I've retraced my steps around Willy's mansion many times since.

I recently helped my brother move house and when cleaning out his loft I uncovered a rubber-keyed Spectrum. My pulse quickened as I imagined it might be *the* Spectrum, the 16K computer our dad brought home in 1983. It wasn't. It was a 48K model my brother had acquired at some point.

He let me have it and that evening I tested it, purely with a view to selling it on. After much fiddling with the TV tuner settings the 'Sinclair Research' screen popped out of the static. Great, it worked and I could sell it. I then tested the tape player and the loading sequence pretty much floored me.

When was the last time I actually loaded a Spectrum game and listened to that abominable sound and watched the screen do its thing rather than loading it instantly through an emulator? I have no idea, but it took me right back to my childhood and it was wonderful.

The Spectrum is going nowhere.

Martyn pictured in 1988. Santa clearly delivered copies of *Barbarian II* and *After Burner* that year.

THE PERIPHERALS

ZX Microdrive

Loading games onto the ZX Spectrum could take forever - the Microdrive was Sinclair's answer to the problem - a device that could format, read and write to 85KB cartridges that slotted into the front of the device. The Microdrive proved unreliable but much faster than standard tape.

ZX Interface 1

The Interface 1 allowed the connection of Microdrive(s) to the ZX Spectrum. It also sported an RS-232 port that allowed a network of Spectrums to be connected together.

ROM Cartridges

Sinclair released the Interface 2 allowing the use of ROM cartridges and two joysticks that adhered to the 'Sinclair' standard. Pictured here is Kempston's version of the interface.

Kempston Joystick Interface

To use a joystick for gaming, a joystick interface was required. Kempston introduced their interface which became a widespread standard in most games.

Alphacom 32 Printer

Sinclair released the ZX Printer and used special 'silver' thermal paper to display printed content. The Alphacom 32 printer was an alternative thermal printer to Sinclair's offering using white paper that proved much more readable.

Dk'Tronics Keyboard

A bugbear of the 48K Spectrum for many of its owners was the keyboard. This Dk'Tronics offering was by far the most popular alternative and cheap at £40.

Dk'Tronics Light Pen

The lightpen was a gimmick more than offering any practical function. When your mates came over to play Manic Miner, you could sort of draw their name on your TV to impress them!

Rotronics Wafadrive

The Wafadrive is an impressive looking bit of kit that performs the same function as the ZX Microdrive but uses 'Wafers' for data storage. The device was known for being slow.

The iconic front
cover of Issue 1 of
Crash magazine
by Oliver Frey.

THE GAMES

CHOOSE TEAM TO MANAGE -	
NUMBER	NAME
1	Arsenal
2	Aston V.
3	Brighton
4	Coventry
5	Everton
6	Ipswich
7	Liverpool
8	Luton
9	Man.City
10	Man.Utd
11	Norwich
12	Notts.F.
13	Swansea
14	Spurs
15	Watford
16	West Ham

Type team number of the team you
want to manage (or 99 for more
choice)

(h=copy)

Name	:	Football Manager
Year	:	1982
Publisher	:	Addictive Games Ltd
Author	:	Kevin J.M. Toms

P = picked to play, i = injured

	NAME	NO.	SKILL	ENERGY	VALUE	
D	P.Parkes	1	3	16	£15000	P
D	D.Watson	2	3	13	£15000	P
D	P.Neal	3	5	14	£25000	P
D	A.Martin	4	1	16	£5000	P
D	K.Sansom	5	1	7	£5000	P
D	R.Osman	7	5	12	£25000	P
M	G.Rix	11	3	13	£15000	P
M	B.Talbot	15	3	8	£15000	
M	S.McCall	16	4	8	£20000	P
A	C.Regis	17	2	9	£10000	P
A	T.Morley	19	2	10	£10000	P
A	K.Keegan	23	1	16	£5000	P

PLAYERS PICKED=11

TYPE NO. OF PLAYER TO BE SOLD
OR type 99 to continue

(h=copy)

When looking back at the origins of the football simulator, it can be said with some degree of certainty that this game is where it all began. The cassette cover has a smiling, bearded man named Kevin, with full Keegan perm, beckoning you to purchase his lovingly crafted BASIC program that challenged the player to ascend a team from the 1982 Football League to the top of the league. By mixing up the skills of the squad before kick-off, the game plays out glorious stick-o-vision highlights that demonstrate the graphical prowess of the early Spectrum games. While watching, it's important to have a beer in one hand and the TV remote in the other whilst shouting 'Shoot, SHOOOOT', at your bumbling striker as he slowly moves towards the goal. If you are lucky, your man scores and it's back to the main menu to start the whole process again. If he doesn't score…well you get the picture. *Football Manager* can still to this day hold your interest for a short while but you soon find yourself relegating the game back to the 4th division where it now belongs.

dk'tronics

Name	:	3D Tanx
Year	:	1982
Publisher	:	Dk'Tronics
Author	:	Don Priestley

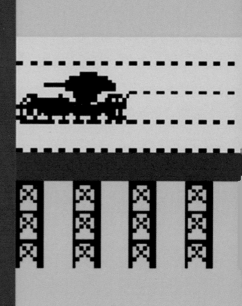

D kTronics *3D Tanx* has a simple premise - kill or be killed. As the game starts you find yourself manning a powerful artillery unit with the ability to move the weapon left or right and its turret up and down. Pressing fire sees a shell fire off into the pseudo 3D landscape and land on a distant bridge. So far nothing too life threatening. From the right a lone tank comes into view and turns its turret and locks on you. BANG - a shot is fired. Quickly you move to the left to dodge the incoming missile - it hits your protective armour. You survive. You fire back - a direct hit disables the enemy. You fire again - the tank is destroyed. You breathe a sigh of relief. Two more tanks trundle onto the bridge, then three, then four. Each time one is destroyed another one rolls into view. Missiles rain in on your position. Kill or be killed - such is the premise of the game. You dodge; you fire; you are awarded points; you die. War has never been this much fun!

sinclair

Name	:	Horace Goes Skiing
Year	:	1982
Publisher	:	Sinclair Research Ltd
Author	:	William Tang

Horace is a handsome chap - if he wasn't popping pills or chasing spiders you could always count on finding him on-piste at the local ski resort. *Horace Goes Skiing* is two games for the price of one. With the popular *Frogger* game raking in the 10p coins in the arcades at the time, the first part of this game sees you controlling Horace across a busy road to get to the slopes. Leg it and hope for the best is the order of the day here, using the green cross code will only get you run over and having to fork out $$ to the same private healthcare vehicle that just run poor Horace down. Likened to crossing the M6 carriageway on a busy bank holiday weekend, survive the ordeal and it's onto the Skiing part of the game. A fine use of the white colour of the Spectrum palette is used for this downhill slalom affair as Horace is guided left and right whilst dodging trees and making jumps that would put Shaun White to shame. Complete the course and it's back to the ski hut again.

SCORE 0 HI 0

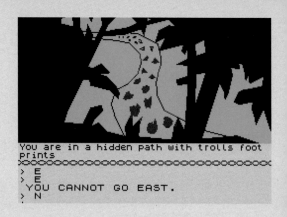

Name	:	The Hobbit
Year	:	1982
Publisher	:	Melbourne House
Author	:	Philip Mitchell, Veronika Megler

When playing *The Hobbit* a vivid imagination is helpful. The game sports simple graphics that depict the location you find yourself occupying - it does help somewhat to mentally add colour to the scene just as you would if you were reading the Tolkien book itself. To help the player fill in the gaps, the game actually came with the book on release and it was paramount for it to be read to have any real idea of what you were trying to do. When playing the game, instructions could be entered similar to natural speech making *The Hobbit* a landmark title in the text adventure space. As the characters made their way independently across Middle Earth, you never quite knew who you were going to bump into on the next input of 'W', 'E', 'N' or 'S'. You waited and time passed. Eventually you find your way to Smaug and defeat him by entering an assortment of commands and become the everlasting hero. If only there was a princess to rescue!

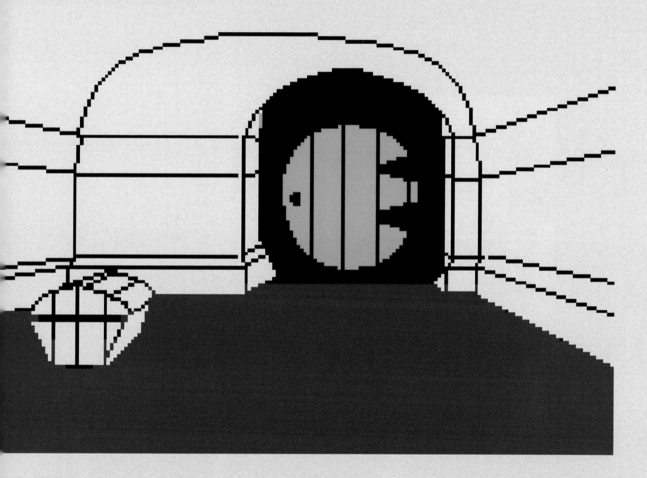

comfortable tunnel like hall

sinclair

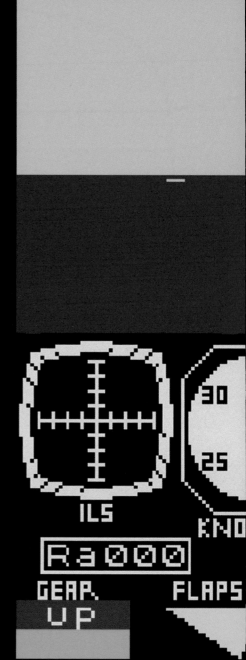

Name	:	Flight Simulation
Year	:	1983
Publisher	:	Sinclair Research
Author	:	Charles Davies

A a thirteen year old lad, the art of flying a plane was beyond my comprehension, involving physics that I had yet to learn. Psion's *Flight Simulation* allowed me to give flying a go and by doing so ensured, that after crashing umpteen times whilst coming into land and taking off, it was not a career I would want to progress after A levels. Written in BASIC the game chugs along at a woeful frame rate and can take some time to represent your intended manoeuvre on the screen. The scenery is non-existent with a few graphical representations of lakes to break up the monotony of blue. Crashing is frequent, albeit in slow motion. Saying 'No' to giving flying one more go, the game jumps into the BASIC program showing off Charles Davies' mathematical code. So far the compliments have not flowed - the reality though with *Flight Simulation* is that with a joystick in hand and the cockpit in front of you, the game gave budding enthusiasts the opportunity to 'simulate' flying and landing a 'huge' carrier. Maybe flying a plane is not that hard.

Megadodo Software

Name	:	Pheenix
Year	:	1983
Publisher	:	Megadodo Software
Author	:	Martin W. Ward

003200

PHEENIX

Superb presentation graphics and sound. Highly recommended. (Home Comp Wkly)
The best Spectrum Pheenix yet! (Software Supermarket)

(Screen 5)

You are in command of the star-destroyer Phoenix. Swarms of robot scout birds attack you. Beautiful eggs magically appear, then hatch into deadly Phoenix war birds. Can you survive to face the heavily guarded flagship?

- 5 screens   • 5 skill levels   • demonstration mode
- full sound effects   • music   • flapping birds
- Kempston & AGF joystick compatible   • 100% m/c

ONLY £5·50
for any 16k or any 48k
ZX SPECTRUM
DEALER ENQUIRIES WELCOME

send cheque/P.O. to
Megadodo Software
16 While Road
Sutton Coldfield
W Midlands B72 1ND

MEGADODO   SOFTWARE

presents

Pheenix

© MEGADODO SOFTWARE 1983
written by M.W.Ward

press 5 to start

emories of seeing the arcade game *Phoenix* for the first time are vivid - it was in the foyer of the local cinema in Carmarthen in West Wales. I used to take my younger sister to see some of the Disney movies that were showing at the time and always walked past the cabinet slowly on the way in trying to get a glimpse of the action, and then used to hover around the machine on the way out watching some of the local teens playing the game and impressing the girls - I was captivated. I daren't play that cabinet for fear of not being very good and humiliating myself in front of the opposite sex. The release of *Pheenix* (see what they did there) on the Spectrum was the answer to my woes - I could practice this faithful production of the game in private and hone my skills. By the time I was good, and confident, enough to go public - the cinema had replaced *Phoenix* with the next big name and my opportunity was lost to impress, what could have been, my future wife. Back to the drawing board.

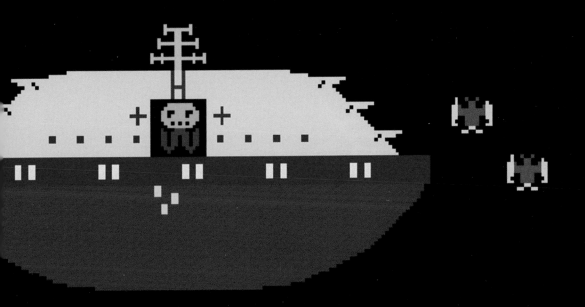

Name	:	Penetrator
Year	:	1983
Publisher	:	Melbourne House
Author	:	Philip Mitchell, Veronika Megler

Stage 2.

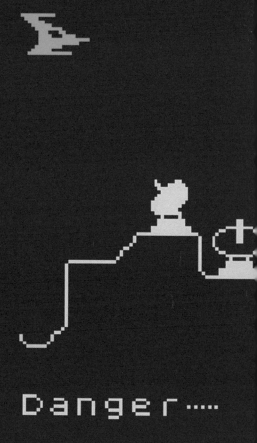

Danger.....

Another firm favourite in the arcades of the time was *Scramble* - and such was the fashion of the time, publishers took inspiration from these games and produced their own interpretation for the home computers. Apart from its dubious name, *Penetrator* was by far the best *Scramble* clone on the ZX Spectrum and faithfully represented each of the cavernous areas of its arcade brethren allowing you to spew bombs onto the undulating ground below and fire torpedoes straight ahead at launching enemies. On clearing a cycle of the game you are rewarded with a firework display that, to this day, challenges those of New Years Eve celebrations in London. The aim of the game was all about beating your high score - and with the addictive qualities of the game kicking in from the word go, many a late night in the 80s resulted in bleary eyed pupils trying to stay awake on arriving at early morning lessons at school. The teacher probably had the very same challenge for the very same reason!

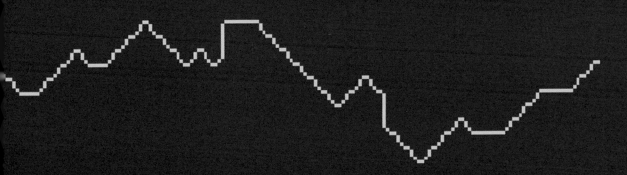

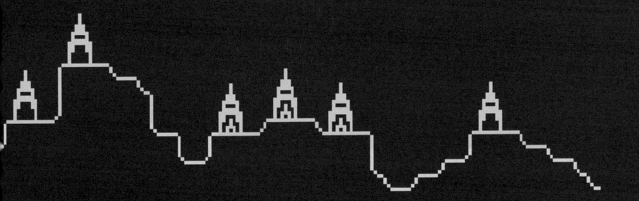

QUICKSILVA

```
**** ANT ATTACK ****
**** SCORE CARD ****

LIVES SAVED :        2

TIME LEFT   :      398

TOTAL SCORE :     1516

So far so good. On your feet
once more...  no time for a
coffee break !
```

Name	:	Ant Attack
Year	:	1983
Publisher	:	Quicksilva
Author	:	Sandy White, Angela Sutherland

SCORE :

ANT ATTACK
FROM
QUICKSILVA

```
QUICKSILVA

  present ...

ANT ATTACK

© SANDY WHITE 1983


SOFT SOLID 3-D Pat.Pending


 Girl or Boy (g/b)?
```

20

AMMO   G

With *Ant Attack*, Sandy White arguably created the first 3D world on the Spectrum. The game lets you choose to be the hero or heroine and it's with some intrepid urgency you go in search of your loved one, kidnapped whilst on their travels in Antescher. The name of the city itself gives a clue to the inhabitants of this walled fortress - huge ants that home in on you for a bite when you get close. When you find the love of your life, it's a matter of shouting 'Follow me!' before racing towards the exit with your partner in tow. If you find yourself disorientated and get cornered in many of the dead ends in the city, the devious ants will club together to secure your demise. Keyboard bashing then ensues in the hope you kill the ants, not yourself, with the many grenades (known for killing ants of the large kind) in your pocket - if you're lucky, you survive. Invariably you blow yourself up! *Ant Attack* is a technical marvel on the Spectrum - often let down by 'blow yourself up' controls.

sinclair

Name	:	Stop The Express
Year	:	1983
Publisher	:	Sinclair Research Ltd
Author	:	Hudson Soft

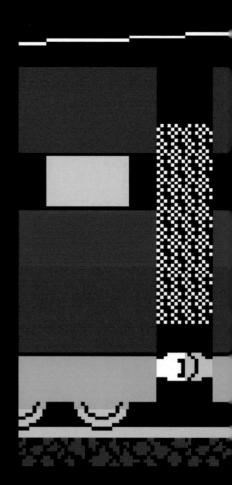

TOP
000200

TOP   SCORE TIME CAR STG
003210 003210 000 255 001

CONGRATURATION♥ YOU SUCSESS♥

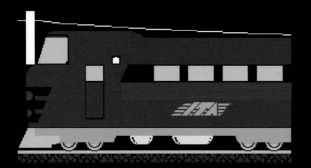

There are many examples of games in the early life of the Spectrum where anything goes. A simple idea is thought of and then a prototype gets created that is continually added to until a game pops out the other side. This seems to be the case with *Stop The Express* - a simple idea of a game where you make your way, dressed in your onesie, from the back to the front of a fast moving train whilst jumping between carriages, dodging the bullets from the 'Redmen' and ducking beneath deadly archways. If you trap the red birds that fly by, you can sho them at the 'Redmen'. Half way along the stretch of carriages, your adventure switches to the inside of the carriages where it's more of the same. With the 'thumpety thump' of the tracks below you eventually reach the front of the tra and receive your just rewards - the train stops! On your quest, if you are hit by any object, inanimate or otherwise, you are knocked off the train and tumble to a premature death. *Stop the Express* is original, frustratingly addictive anc downright thrilling.

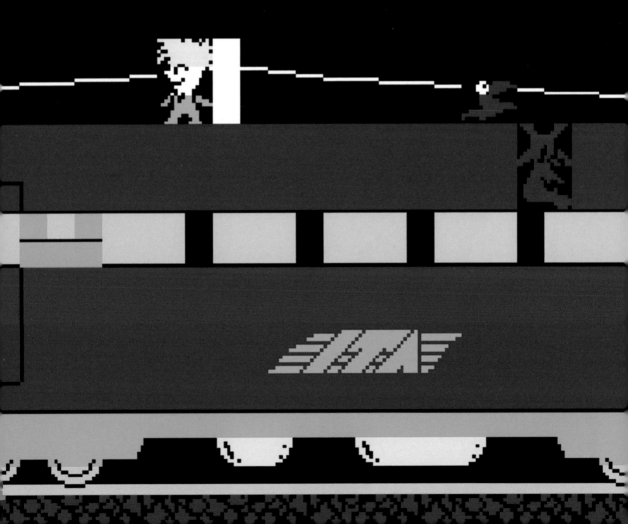

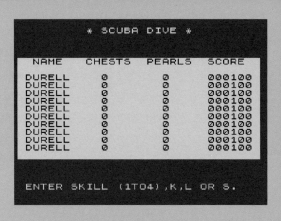

NAME	CHESTS	PEARLS	SCORE
DURELL	0	0	000100
DURELL	0	0	000100
DURELL	0	0	000100
DURELL	0	0	000100
DURELL	0	0	000100
DURELL	0	0	000100
DURELL	0	0	000100
DURELL	0	0	000100
DURELL	0	0	000100
DURELL	0	0	000100

ENTER SKILL (1TO4),K,L OR S.

Name	:	Scuba Dive
Year	:	1983
Publisher	:	Durell Software
Author	:	Mike A. Richardson

Pushing yourself off the back of your boat is the start of an incredible adventure into the depths of the inky black ocean, on the lookout for pearls hundreds of metres beneath the surface. Sounds pretty straightforward until you realise you are not alone - brilliantly animated sea creatures, such as the cuddly Great White shark, fill the world beneath the waves and help to deplete your oxygen if you so much as touch one of their pixels with your not so protective scuba outfit. Oxygen tanks can be found in the deepest caves - if you're desperate your tank can be replenished by surfacing and getting back onto your boat which invariably has been taken for a jolly by the skipper. You score points for pearls brought back to the boat, the deeper you venture the more points you get for each find - if you get knocked out by various baddies or even eaten then your pearls are lost to the deep forever. *Scuba Dive* is another highly original game by the Durell team that proves to be highly therapeutic as well as fun.

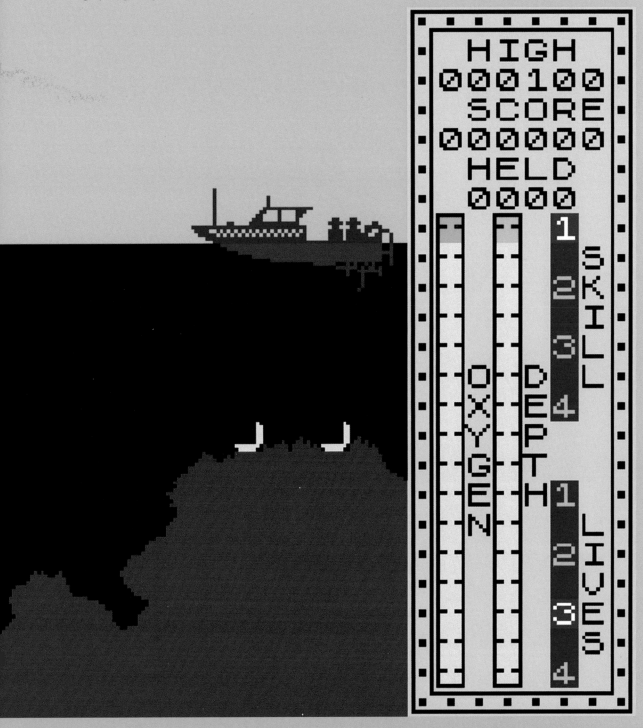

JETPAC GAME SELECTION

1   1 PLAYER GAME
2   2 PLAYER GAME
3   KEYBOARD
4   KEMPSTON JOYSTICK

5   START GAME

1UP
001275

Name	:	Jetpac
Year	:	1983
Publisher	:	Ultimate Play The Game
Author	:	Tim Stamper, Chris Stamper

JETPAC IS LOADING.

Ultimate Play the Game became the company to beat very early on in the life of the ZX Spectrum with stunning titles that other developers had to live up to – they became the benchmark with each new title released. *Jetpac* was their first title, released in 1983 for the lowly 16K Spectrum, where your protagonist space adventurer is thrust into intergalactic travel, building spaceships, killing aliens and trying to figure out the meaning of life. The game's objective is simple; build your spaceship, fill it with fuel then rocket on to the next level, all the while dodging an array of technicolor aliens. The mechanics of the game are sublime – using '*Jetpac* Thrustpack' technology (trademark pending), Jetman bounds across the screen with graceful inertia-based aplomb. With a gentle squeeze of the fire button, a satisfyingly vibrant laser burst is sent across the screen, vaporising anything in its path. With the clearance of each screen, the player's score thrusts forward – one more go on this game is never enough, as you try to beat your all time high score.

	1	KEYBOARD
	2	KEMPSTON JOYSTICK
	3	CURSOR JOYSTICK
	4	KNIGHT
	5	WIZARD
	6	SERF
	0	START GAME

Name	:	Atic Atac
Year	:	1983
Publisher	:	Ultimate Play The Game
Author	:	Tim Stamper, Chris Stamper

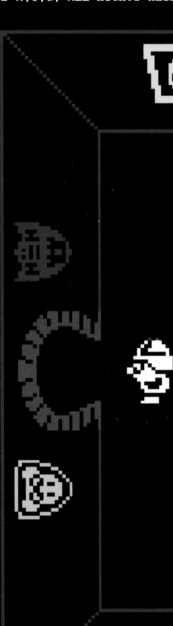

Once upon a time, 3D graphics were the stuff of fancy. They were viewed as some far off fantasy that may never come true, but irrepressible dreamers like the Stamper brothers worked hard to bring such things to the waking world. *Atic Atac* successfully placed gamers within a seemingly-real castle, and embellished on its remarkable realism with a powerful narrative and some revolutionary gameplay mechanics. Most notably you could choose from three different playable characters - a wizard, knight or a serf - and each one came with its own unique journey during the quest to find the mysterious Golden Key of ACG, and thence the castle escape. Pieces of this key were squirreled about the enemy-laden castle, as you attempt to run through the randomly-opening and closing doors, avoiding being trapped for too long in a dangerous place. Of particular note were the gravestones of previously fallen characters, which remained in place throughout subsequent games and marked your previous progress.

Name	:	Manic Miner
Year	:	1983
Publisher	:	Bug-Byte Software / Software Projects
Author	:	Matthew Smith

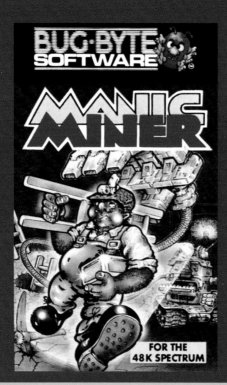

6

031769 is etched into the brain waves of many a retro gamer. This sequence of numbers activated level select on Bug-Byte's version of *Manic Miner*, giving the player half a chance to see and play the later levels of Matthew Smith's 20-level *Miner 2049er* inspired game. Miner Willy is the star and sees the player guiding him through each screen collecting keys that open up the door to the next level. Sounds simple – the challenge comes from the myriad of madcap enemies that are intent on taking Willy's life; killer penguins, mutant telephones, snapping toilets and, well, odd looking things protect each level and traverse back and forth relentlessly along set paths. Timing is the name of the game – with no weapon to remove the pixelated nasties, jumps have to be pixel perfect to ensure avoiding contact with anything that moves. As you hum along to 'In The Hall of the Mountain King' playing in a rhythmic loop as you play, you lose your last life and a Pythonesque foot squishes poor Willy. Time to type in 6031769 again!

Name	:	Deathchase
Year	:	1983
Publisher	:	Micromega
Author	:	Mervyn J. Estcourt, R.B

One of the most exhilarating scenes within the Star Wars movie 'The Return of the Jedi' is the chase through the forests of Endor on the Speeder Bikes where Luke is hunting down some of the Imperial scum after they spotted him having Rebel shenanigans with Leia. *3D Deathchase* was as close as you were going to get to being on Endor as you guide your bike through a lush woodland area at breathtaking speed, avoiding the trees and shooting multi-coloured shots at enemies who, as is always the case in games, have their reasons for seeing your termination. For the time, *Deathchase* was cutting edge aggressive gameplay in a 16K wrapper. Graphically the game is nothing to write home about – but the sense of hi-octane speed was unparalleled in 1983 as you screamed through the 14 levels of forestation, gunning down tanks, helicopters and other bikers as day turned to night, for no other apparent reason other than brazen entertainment. Often voted in the top 5 of every Spectrum fans list of greatness, *3D Deathchase* still delivers oodles of fun.

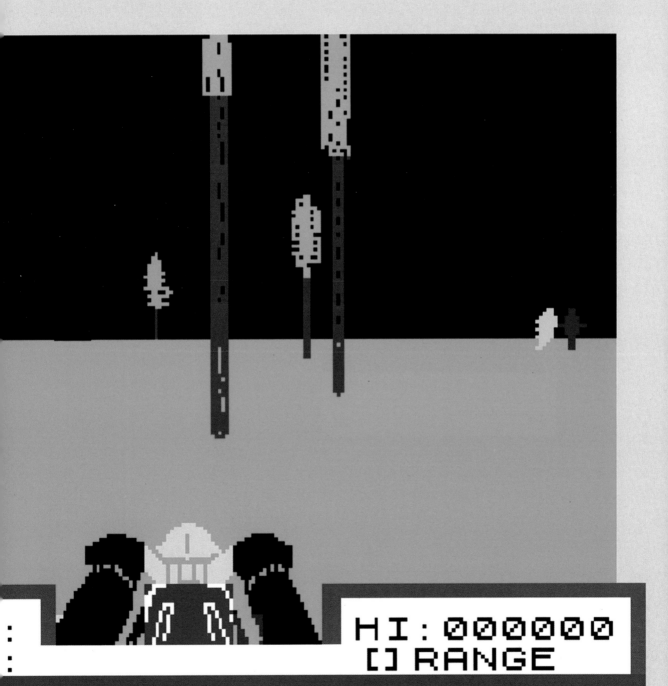

QUICKSILVA

TIME·GATE

BY JOHN HOLLIS

TRAINING
MANUAL
© QUICKSILVA

J oin me on a journey through time, before YouTube reviews and playable demos and decades before the Internet of today. Travel further back, before movie tie-ins and sequels. Way back to when games were truly original, before the Big Bang of releases overwhelmed our game buying decisions. Back then you invested time in each game - partly because they took so long to load. In *4D Time-Gate*, as the wonderful backstory will attest, you have to travel in space and time to vanquish 'The Enemy' before they struck their first blow. My brother and I played it for hours at a time, exploring, shooting, 'jumping' - leaving the laser beams temporarily frozen in time. We completed it more than once; to us, it was Firebird's *Elite* and Cameron's Terminator combined, but the game predated both. Quicksilva subsequently published numerous unique, often overlooked classics, many of which we owned. *Time-Gate* was one of five games that my brother and I had to select, without reviews or screenshots. They were bundled with our Spectrum, purchased from Dixons in October and finally unwrapped on Christmas Day, 1983.

Gareth Perch

EVEL ONE
ELECTED
LL SYSTEMS
PERATIONAL

PRESENTS

ZZOOM

BY JOHN GIBSON

Copyright: Program,Audio,Visual
© 1983 by IMAGINE SOFTWARE

PRESS ANY KEY TO BEGIN

Name	:	Zzoom
Year	:	1983
Publisher	:	Imagine Software
Author	:	John Gibson, Steve Blower, Mark Butler

zzoom is loading
PLEASE WAIT

With a title that has us humming along to a song similarly titled by Fat Larry's Band, *Zzoom* (please note the extra Z) finds the player defending a group of waving refugees waiting for rescue. There is an element of urgency here as planes swoop in over land, tanks fire unceremoniously at you from the desert and submarines look to take you out by sea. In your defence you have an artillery gun in the shape of a cross hair that can be moved around the screen, in the first person, to target and shoot the foe. Let's not forget the refugees – they are the innocent ones caught up in this unwieldy battle and fly into the air with acrobatic grace if hit in the crossfire. A talking point at the time was that if you were feeling a little vindictive, you could aim your crossfire onto the little fellas and well, if the mood took, you could press fire! A refugee is saved by simply protecting them long enough for them to walk on, and then off the playing area. Maybe this is a game that could be updated with Oculus Rift Virtual Reality compatibility.?

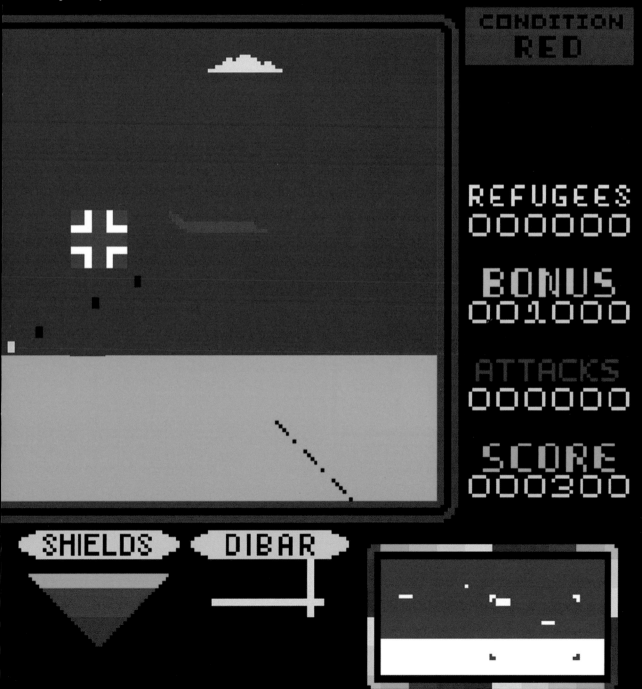

MICROSPHERE

Name   :   Wheelie
Year   :   1983
Publisher   :   Microsphere
Author   :   David S. Reidy and Keith Warrington

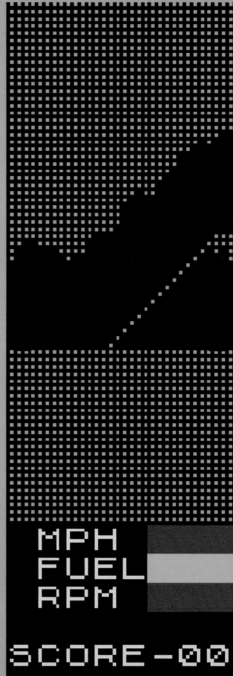

B ack in the 80's, Kick Start was a huge TV phenomenon where kids used their biking and balancing skills to traverse a scramble course of barrels, logs and ramps all in the name of entertainment. *Wheelie* could be accused of jumping on the bandwagon somewhat and using a similar formula, but look a little closer and you will find an endearing game with a dark and foreboding edge. There you are, out on the roads one stormy night on your Zedexaki 500 superbike and you inadvertently enter Nightmare Park, a maze of side-scrolling dead ends, abandoned buses and jumps. Your aim is to escape this 'nightmare' – find the Ghost Rider (obviously) and race him to the park entrance and eternal freedom. *Wheelie* is a technological marvel for the time but can be a difficult game to play. Mastering the controls and the behaviour of your bike results in a hugely enjoyable experience, mixing that of trial-biking and stunt performing (remember Eddie Kidd was doing some rather mental things at the time!).

Name	:	Jumping Jack
Year	:	1983
Publisher	:	Imagine Software
Author	:	Albert Ball, Stuart C. Ball

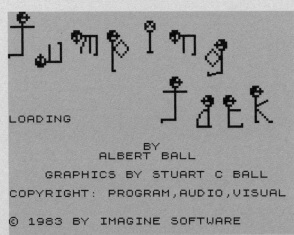

LOADING

BY
ALBERT BALL
GRAPHICS BY STUART C BALL
COPYRIGHT: PROGRAM,AUDIO,VISUAL
© 1983 BY IMAGINE SOFTWARE

Jumping Jack is about as minimal as gaming can get. Stick man hero Jack is well named, since jumping is all he can do. Your goal is to get him to the top of the screen, through six platforms. Hit a platform from beneath, and Jack is knocked out and loses a life. Instead, you must wait for the gaps in the platforms – just two to begin with – to make their way around to where you are. When you get to the top of the screen, you earn two lines from Jack's limerick, and then start over with more gaps. While that makes it easier to ascend, it also makes it easier to fall back down. That's really all there is to *Jumping Jack*, a true relic of Speccy gaming's first awkward years, but that doesn't mean it's without merit. On the contrary, with its simple rules and moreish 'one last go' appeal it's a direct ancestor of today's mobile hits. *Doodle Jump* owes much to games like *Jumping Jack,* and the gameplay in particular is basically *Flappy Bird*, thirty years before *Flappy Bird* was a thing. It may not be much to look at, but there's a primal allure to games like this that shines through even the most basic graphics.

HI00045   SC00015

Thor arrives.
Thor congratulates you.
Thor leaves.

Name	:	Valhalla
Year	:	1983
Publisher	:	Legend
Author	:	Richard Edwards, Graham Asher,
		Charles Goodwin, Andrew Owen

You are i
an area o

£14.99 for a game I hear you shout! Yep, that is how much *Valhalla* cost to buy back in the day – its saving grace was that it, erm, came in a nice big, black box that had a large Viking head on it. Striking! Inside though was just a cassette tape and a flimsy instruction manual just like its £5.95 brethren. *Valhalla* did try to be theatrically different though – written primarily in BASIC, the graphical adventure depicts huge castle scenes and gives the illusion of a real time land reminiscent of the lands of Mordor. Interaction with the game is via a clever parser that can even understand rude words, which when predictably entered (just testing to make sure the game works mum!) sees a Dwarf come onto the screen and punch the player's character. The main aim of the game is to collect six mythical objects scattered around the land and on your travels you meet an assortment of wonderful and varied characters. As you are pondering your next move, it is quite disconcerting to see the game carrying on without your input – this does beg the question of your role in the game.

Valheim, which is in
lakes in Asgard.

New Generation Software

Name	:	Trashman
Year	:	1984
Publisher	:	New Generation Software
Author	:	Malcolm E. Evans

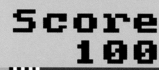

Score
100

© NEW GENERATION SOFTWARE

T*rashman* is a game that proves that anything can be fun and inspirational game ideas are all around us - you just have to open your eyes. *Trashman* takes the concept of collecting rubbish from the houses in a well-to-do sub urban area and making it fun. You, as the bin-collector, have to navigate your way up a busy street emptying the contents of bins (no 'green bins for this' and 'blue bins for that' in this game) in to your garbage collector (bin lorry if you are in the UK). All the while you have to dodge angry dogs (who obviously slept in and missed the postman that morning) protecting their owner's property, boy racers that ignore the 30mph legal speed limit and keep up with a very keen bin wagon driver who just wants to get home for his tea. Compliments have to go to the author of this game for making, what seems on the face of it, a mundane task into an enjoyable, challenging romp. What a fantastically 'rubbish' game.

FIREBIRD

Name	:	Booty
Year	:	1984
Publisher	:	Firebird
Author	:	John F. Cain

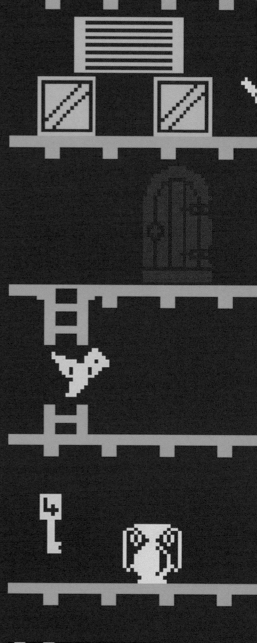

When thinking of *Booty* you could be forgiven for thinking these days of Beyonce or maybe Jennifer Lopez. I digress. The kind of *Booty* that this game references is the type pirates look for within the caves of islands far, far away. That's it, treasure me 'arties. Fundamentally a platformer, *Booty* was the first title released by Telecomsoft on their budget Firebird label and sees you, the cabin boy, making your way through the ship's holds. Each step of the way is blocked by doors that are opened by finding the correctly numbered key in the hold. In total there are 20 holds to explore and there is plenty of loot to be collected on the way as you hum along to that well known shanty tune 'Barnacle Bill' (or more commonly known as the tune from Blue Peter) relentlessly looping in the background. Plug in a Currah μSpeech into the back of your Spectrum before you load the game and an alternative adventure is loaded – one where you explore the depths of the sea collecting small fish. Bargain!

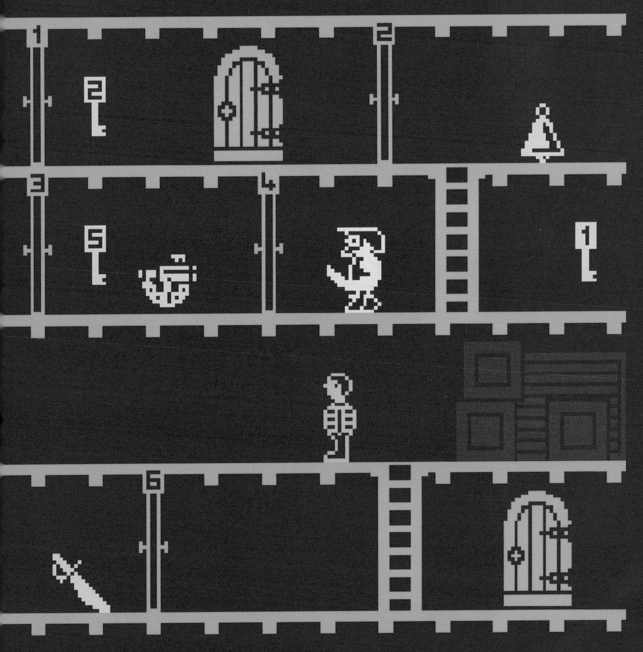

Name	:	Avalon
Year	:	1984
Publisher	:	Hewson Consultants
Author	:	Steve Turner

On reading the review in Sinclair User where they gave the game a mighty nine out of ten, *Avalon* was a must purchase - the promise of a 3D adventure likening you as a hero in the latest Indie-type blockbuster was an invitation that could not be passed. The game came in a video cassette style box and on opening, out fell an obligatory adventurer's map and a set of instructions that hinted that the game was a little more complex than it actually was. Maroc the wizard (or to be precise his astral projection) had to be guided through some pseudo 3D rooms in search of Lord Chaos (cue insane laughter) in order to kill him. Spells and the like are collected to aid the journey. The 3D rooms flicker in motion sickness inducing fashion as you float Maroc through each one – banging into doors (strangely) to open them and generally avoiding foe that chase you, waving their weapons, across the dungeon rooms. *Avalon* is an early cinematic fare that certainly lives up to the brash promises of its accompanying literature - it's just like being Indiana Jones but with a Wizard's hat and staff.

Name	:	Bruce Lee
Year	:	1984
Publisher	:	U.S. Gold
Author	:	L.T. Software for Ocean Software

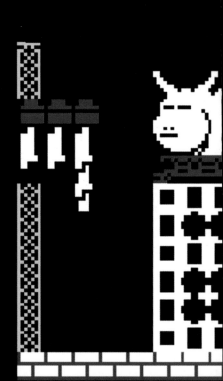

Bruce Lee brings back many fond memories of playing the Speccy with my sister Jenny. Our father allowed us to play it during his breaks from trying to program games and we played it to death using the 2-player option. Taking turns and repeatedly dying when a poorly timed jump ends with an arrow in the head or when those blasted sprouting electric traps kill you after being sent flying from a hit by the Sumo guy. It was equally frustrating as it was enjoyable. The delight of going from room to room collecting yellow lanterns and to progress by climbing, jumping, ducking, running on conveyor belts, jumping mice type lumps and constantly fighting the Ninja and Sumo wrestler (4 successive flying kicks should do it) for 20 rooms, all to defeat the evil Fire Wizard to then start again from the beginning. Memorable levels were wonderfully varied yet simple and the design so iconic for us that it will forever be synonymous with happy times playing the Spectrum in our glorious 48K youth. Oh, and that damn music thankfully didn't go beyond the title screen.

Gary Phillips

Name	:	Sabre Wulf
Year	:	1984
Publisher	:	Ultimate Play The Game
Author	:	Tim Stamper, Chris Stamper

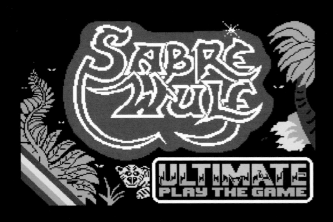

Who's afraid of the big bad wolf? Ultimate had already garnered itself a reputation for releasing some pretty superb titles up to this point, but their Sabreman series would take the bar even higher – *Sabre Wulf* alone reportedly sold in excess of 350,000 copies. It's time for Sabreman to hit the lush primary Spectrum colours of the jungle in search of four ancient amulet pieces. Nasties in the form of spiders, scorpions, parrots and hippos materialize out of nowhere and take a timely swipe of the sword to stun or send them onto their maker. Bumping into the majestic Wulf sees Sabreman coming face to face with a vicious foe that does not think twice about jumping up and down on his poor body. Help comes in the form of special orchids, that if collected, provide power-ups in the form of invincibility and speed-ups. Pick the wrong type of flower and Sabreman can get a little disoriented and respond in reverse to player controls. As the first in a series of games featuring our intrepid hero, *Sabre Wulf* starts Sabreman on a winning streak.

1 KEYBOARD
2 KEMPSTON JOYSTICK
3 CURSOR JOYSTICK
4 INTERFACE II
0 START GAME

Name	:	Underwurlde
Year	:	1984
Publisher	:	Ultimate Play The Game
Author	:	Tim Stamper, Chris Stamper

*U*nderwurlde continues the adventures of *Sabre Wulf's* Sabreman and sees our intrepid hero shooting assorted weapons at carnivorous plants and colourful enemies that are intent on his destruction, whilst collecting assorted treasure across a 597-strong flip-screen maze. Leaping about across undulating caverns, *Underwurlde* gives the player a unique thrill compared to its brethren in the series. While you can come a cropper from falling too far, extra lives and 'blue' invincibility pills give Sabreman half a chance of succeeding in his mission to find the gateway to the follow-up *Knight Lore*, the disappointing *Pentagram* or the unreleased *Mire Mare*. This clever 8-bit game even remembers the position of baddies moving about between nearby screens, which is more than any *Grand Theft Auto* title could do before GTA4! 30 years on, it's quite easy to forget how difficult *Underwurlde* can be; a game that often feels like the forgotten brother - the one that got lost in the mix between the trailblazing success of *Sabre Wulf* and the game-defining isometric 3D titles that followed.   Dom Robinson, DVDfever.co.uk

Name	:	3D Starstrike
Year	:	1984
Publisher	:	Realtime Games Software
Author	:	Ian Oliver, Andrew Onions, Graeme Baird

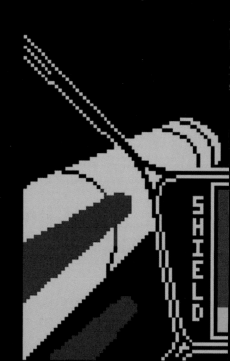

Star Wars euphoria spilled over into the arcades of the '80s with Atari launching their iconic *Star Wars* cockpit cabinet into the bustling seaside arcades and pleasing so many wannabe Jedi Knights eager to take on the dark side of the force and ultimately blow the hell out of the Deathstar. *3D Starstrike* brought that experience into the bedroom where the Kempston joystick became the yoke of the iconic X-Wing fighter and the screen of your trusted Ferguson Colour TV became the outer regions of space filled with the Tie Fighter scum of the dark side. With Obi-Wan urging you to 'use the force', wave after wave of vector ships are shot down, laser turrets on sprawling landscapes obliterated and fortified trenches traversed leading you up nicely to the showdown with the Deathstar equivalent. As you shout 'Let's blow this thing and go home', you shoot at two vector boxes that release a force field allowing you through, a somewhat anti-climatic galactic experience to an otherwise flawless tribute to its arcade brethren.

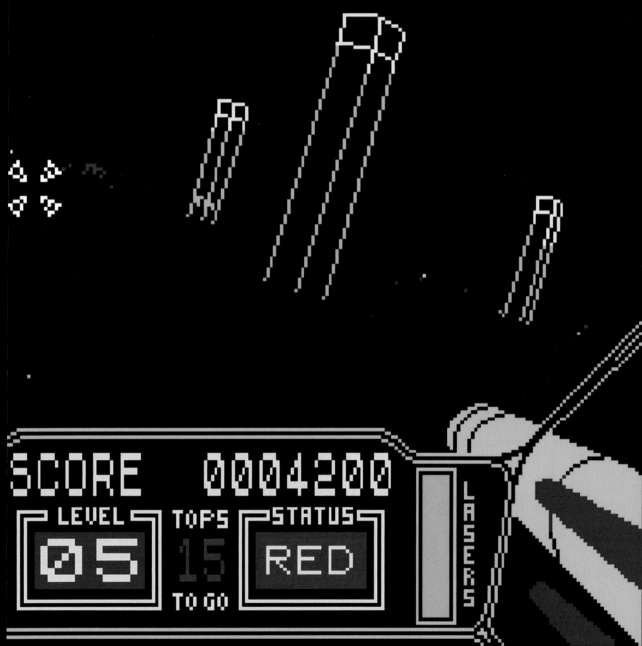

DALEY THOMPSON'S

DECATHLON

1 KEYBOARD
2 KEMPSTON INTERFACE
3 PROTEK INTERFACE
4 SINCLAIR INTERFACE
5 DEMO

WRITTEN BY
P OWENS AND C URQUHART

Name : Daley Thompson's Decathlon

Year : 1984

Publisher : Ocean Software

Author : Paul Owens, Christian F. Urquhart,
F. David Thorpe

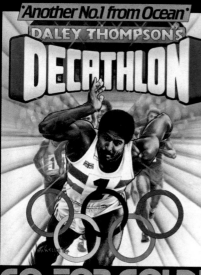

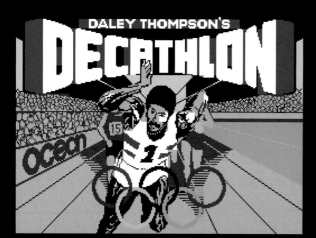

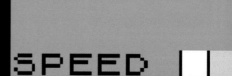

Daley Thompson was a British National Hero back in 1984 and this Ocean game paid tribute to a good number of the events that he competed in at the Los Angeles Olympics. The mechanics and look of the game lent itself to the popular *Track and Field* game that was riding high in the arcades at the time. Many a Quickshot joystick was broken by the avid bedroom athlete as they 'waggled' their stick left and right whilst willing the 'white' Daley character on the screen to go faster. The 110m Hurdles, Javelin, Pole Vault, Discus, Shot Putt, Long Jump and the High Jump events added a little variety to the running formula where pressing the fire button determined the angle of attack, throw or jump. Daley is given three chances to qualify on each event – qualification sees the crowd roar as the main man takes one step closer to Olympic Gold. Fail, and it's back to the training ground and a hypothetical four-year wait for the next chance.

Name   :   Knight Lore
Year   :   1984
Publisher   :   Ultimate Play The Game
Author   :   Tim Stamper, Chris Stamper

Ultimate Play The Game stir a myriad of emotional connections dating back to the golden years of the 8-Bit home computer revolution. An unsaturated market enabled an array of truly innovative games to be developed that pushed both design and technological boundaries. A time when Ultimate prospered and captured imaginations like no other. Shortly before Christmas, an old school friend confessed to me that he'd found the hidden location of his presents. Whilst mindful that they could return at any time he retrieved from his treasure trove a black box that he handed to me. I was stunned. I'd seen full-page advertisements in Crash magazine with the same cover art. Ultimate were renowned for the secrecy surrounding their titles. Due to this clever strategy, anticipation for any Ultimate game was immense. The year was 1984, *Knight Lore* had been unleashed and Sabreman was back for his third instalment! It resembled nothing that I'd played before. The groundbreaking isometric graphics were just spellbinding and created a genre that would be defined in history forever. Play The Ultimate Game. I did.

Mike Parkes

Top Landing

Items collected 000 Time 7:01am

Name	:	Jet Set Willy
Year	:	1984
Publisher	:	Software Projects
Author	:	Matthew Smith

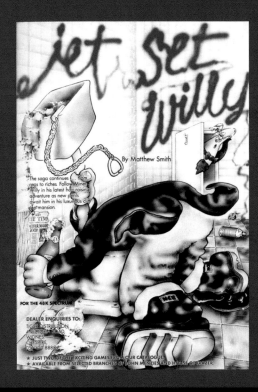

+++++ Press ENTER to Start +++++

The wonderful, warped mind of Matthew Smith sees a return in *Jet Set Willy* where Miner Willy, our enduring hero, is trying to get to bed after a pretty full-on party at his 60-room mansion. His housekeeper is not too impressed with the after-party carnage and sends Willy on his way to clear up the mess before he can rest. And so your adventure begins – a huge sprawling re-imagining of everything that made the prequel, *Manic Miner*, so special and much, much more. Each room has a new assortment of enemies to consider –razor blades; flying pigs; floating barrels; alien blobs; cutting saws to name but a few. Matthew was under pressure to get the game released by Software Projects and as a result a number of glaring bugs were introduced (which were passed off as features initially) which meant the game could not be completed. A number of POKESs later and the flaws were corrected. Spectrum Fact #96: The game was number one in the charts for months, that is until *Sabre Wulf* was released.

Name	:	The Lords of Midnight
Year	:	1984
Publisher	:	Beyond Software
Author	:	Mike Singleton

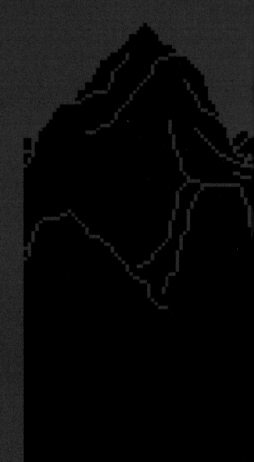

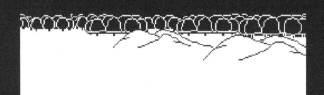

The late, great Mike Singleton never thought small, and when you look at what went into his epic 1984 fantasy opus, *Lords of Midnight*, you could be forgiven for mistaking it for an entry in the vast openworld role-playing games of *The Elder Scrolls* series. Using a graphical technique called 'landscaping' to create a realistic environment of hundreds of locations that could be viewed from eight different directions, this was arguably the first game to truly create a living breathing world to explore. And explore you must, as you control four characters seeking to defeat the evil Doomdark. You can play the game more as an adventure, following the story and destroying Doomdark's crown, or as a game of strategy and diplomacy, recruiting the land's many different factions and plotting an enormous military campaign in order to sway the balance of power and bring down Doomdark's forces. With its open-ended gameplay and emphasis on forging alliances, *Lords of Midnight* represents the early flourishing of themes Singleton would explore in later games, such as *Dark Sceptre* and the 16-bit classic, *Midwinter*.

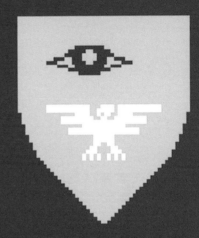

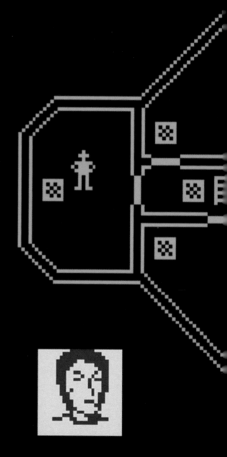

Name	:	Alien
Year	:	1984
Publisher	:	Mind Games
Author	:	John Heap, Paul Clansey

The difficulty of finding a decent movie-to-game adaptation is nothing new, though it certainly still plagues the games industry. Even in 1984 the games media found itself surprised when a faithful and enjoyable tie-in game appeared, and *Alien* was one of the first to accomplish this apparently difficult medium migration. Although it appeared some years after the classic sci-fi/horror flick, it was apparent that the game had been made by dedicated fans of the source material. It didn't cherry pick from franchise and clone whatever types of game were popular at the time. This was an early example of being able to actually play through the events of the movie, and it still stands proud among successful tie-ins today. All the tension and suspense of Alien was captured beautifully, as you guide the terrified crew of the Nostromo around its dark and sinister corridors in an attempt to hunt down the vicious, eponymous xenomorph. It even requires you to save Jones the cat before escaping in the shuttle. How's that for staying true to the original story?

CHUCKIE EGG ©

A GAME
OF SKILL FOR
1 TO 4 PLAYERS
BY N.ALDERTON

FOR INSTRUCTIONS ♦ PRESS S TO

Name	:	Chuckie Egg
Year	:	1984
Publisher	:	A'n'F Software
Author	:	Nigel Alderton

SCORE 0027

PLAYER 1 LEV

THERE'S TROUBLE AT T'FARM!

USE FOUR DIRECTION KEYS WITH
A JUMP KEY TO GUIDE YOUR MAN
AND COLLECT A DOZEN EGGS
YOU MAY CHANGE THE DIRECTION
AND JUMP KEYS. THERE ARE ALSO
THE FOLLOWING FIXED KEYS
CAPS SHIFT & H........HOLD
CAPS SHIFT & A.......ABORT

H en-House Harry, now there's a name, is our egg-gathering protagonist who has the task of running through eight barns, collecting a dozen eggs in each. The hens that inhabit each of the buildings are pure evil and will peck Harry's eyes out as good as look at him. It may be because, as well as nicking their eggs, their food scattered around the levels is nabbed by our hero as he runs past as well. It's not made clear what is going to happen with all the collected eggs and seed – maybe a gigantic crunchy chicken omelette to whet the appetite. It's also questionable why a giant caged duck hangs precariously at the top left of the screen. Play through the levels and the duck is freed, only to chase you around the screen with more venom than the chickens. *Chuckie Egg* is frantic fun and if anyone asks, the game was created on the ZX Spectrum first not the BBC Micro as many a retro gamer will have you believe – somehow over time, this detail got 'scrambled'.

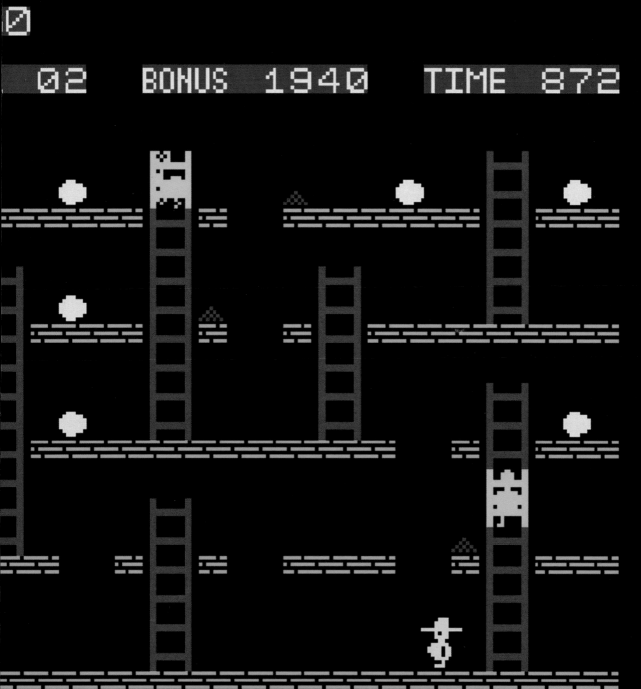

sinclair

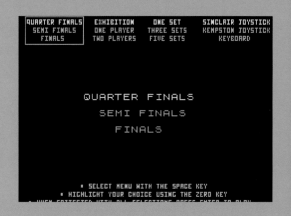

Name	:	Match Point
Year	:	1984
Publisher	:	Sinclair Research Ltd
Author	:	Psion Software Ltd - Steve Kelly

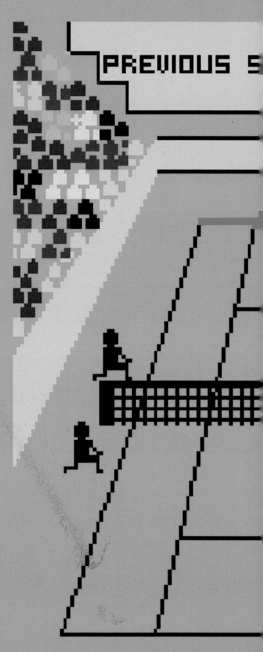

When talk of Wimbledon comes around on the TV you know that Summer has just arrived and that the finest athletes of this prestigious gentleman's club are about to descend on the South East of London and grunt their way through as many sets as they possibly can, all in the name of tennis. *Matchpoint* is a great representation of the sport and allows you, as the player, to get some well needed practice via an exhibition match, or to jump in and play in a competition where winning each round could ultimately see you lifting the trophy, hypothetically speaking. Selecting the skill level changes the aggressiveness of your opponent considerably and at the highest setting you will initially wonder how it's remotely possible just to return a ball, less winning a match. Familiarity of the controls enables you to add speed, direction and accuracy to each of your shots and eventually win your first game. With the smell of freshly cut grass in the air, lifting that trophy in front of royalty will soon be within your grasp.

Game : T.L.L.

Year : 1984

Publisher : Vortex Software

Author : Costa Panayi

TORNADO LOW LEVEL   PRESS ANY KEY

ornado Low Level is an incredible technical marvel on the ZX Spectrum and that's a fact. At the start of the game you find yourself in your hi-tech war plane at the end of the runway, waiting for it to be fuelled. If you're feeling brave (stupid) you could take off before your fuel gauge says full, but it's not recommended as your plane will no doubt come down in a residential area causing all sorts of problems for the locals. Your challenge once airborne is to fly low over the 3D landscape collecting targets – we are talking very low here, so low you could pick flowers from the front porches of the resident's housing and hand them to your loved one on a romantic night out. As well as houses you have pylons, hills and trees to manoeuvre past whilst hunting down each target – in some cases they lurk in the most awkward of locations and prove tricky to gather up. Gorgeous, absorbing and immensely addictive – *T.L.L.* is technically and visually astounding.

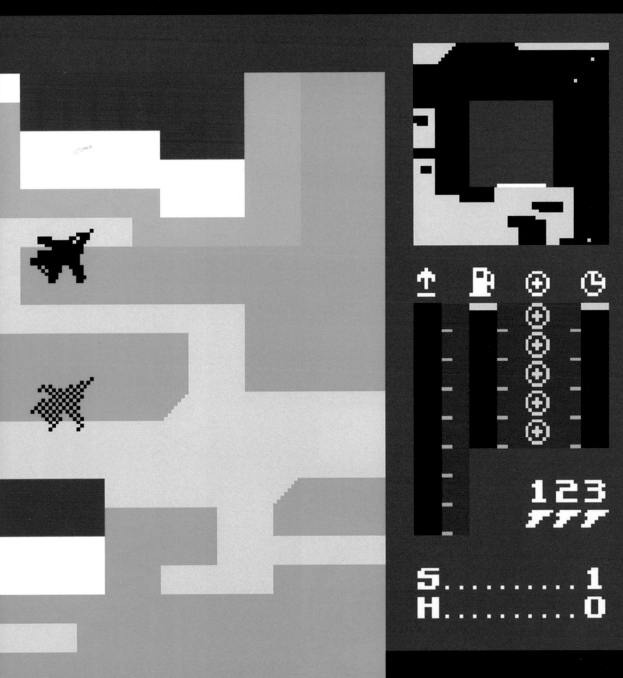

Melbourne House

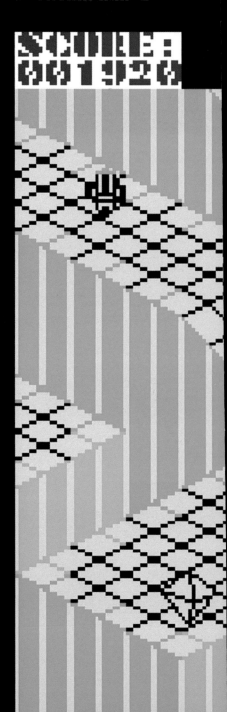

0 – KEYBOARD
1 – KEMPSTON
2 – CURSOR
3 – INTERFACE 2

Name   :   Gyroscope
Year   :   1985
Publisher   :   Melbourne House
Author   :   Steve Lamb, Tony Mack, Dave Dew,
                     Mark Alexander

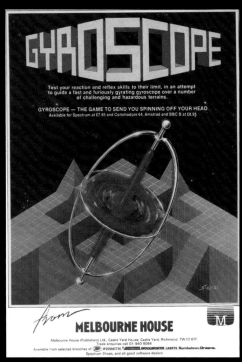

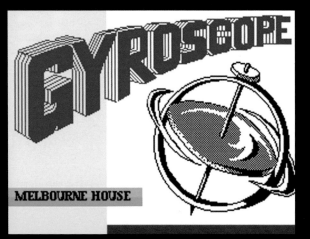

Marble Madness had showcased in the arcades and been deemed a huge success by those that frequented the seaside destinations. With a trackball you had to manoeuvre a ball through a pseudo-3D terrain to the exit whilst dodging various objects that homed in on you with the intent of disrupting your journey. *Gyroscope* took this successful formula and applied it to the home market. The game requires a gyroscope to be guided to the exit dodging meanies, traversing narrow ledges and avoiding being obliterated by falling off the terrain into bottomless canyons. Without the luxury of a trackball, the Quickshot 2 Turbo was the clumsy substitute and increase the difficulty of an already challenging game ten-fold. The game requires huge concentration for success - the startlin sound effects that spew out of the mono sound chip are enough to induce a coronary as 'Gyro' is bounced off another ledge or contact is made with some of the questionable locals. An excellent Spectrum title, check out the great music between levels as well.

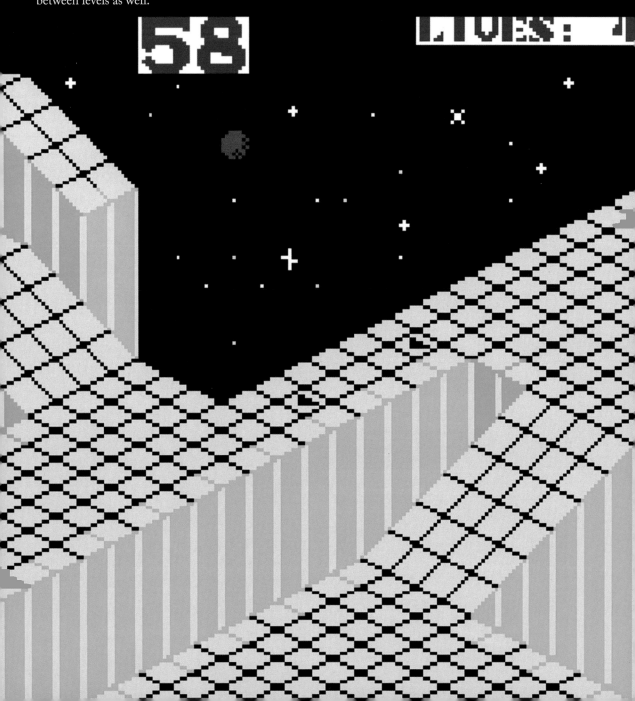

Name	:	Starquake
Year	:	1985
Publisher	:	Bubble Bus Software
Author	:	Stephen J. Crow

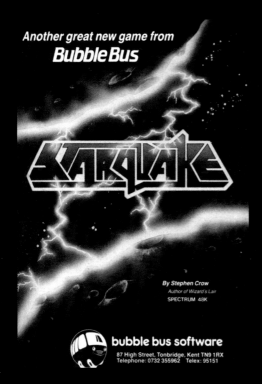

Many a budding bedroom programmer would look at the games coming out of the Ultimate Play The Game sausage factory with envy – every game had been a surefire fit, and there was nothing to suggest that future sausages would not taste as good. *Starquake* gives a nod and a wink to the style, presentation and playability of a typical Ultimate game and sees B.L.O.B. (Bio-Logically Operated Being) crash land his ship on an unknown world. What is evident is that the landing has destablised the planet and to save it from destruction B.L.O.B. has to find pieces of the planet core that have been scattered around the 512 screens of a graphically impressive planet. As you can imagine, the thought of losing their colourful home has upset the locals and they are intent on depleting your life, even though you are trying to make things right. Ask any Spectrum fan their top five games and *Starquake* always features – a tough game with clever puzzles and fantastic sound and an utter charm to play. You cannot help but fall in love with B.L.O.B.

MICROSPHERE

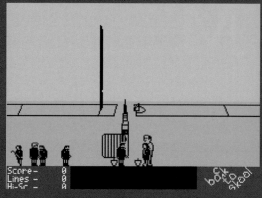

Name	:	Back to Skool
Year	:	1985
Publisher	:	Microsphere
Author	:	David S. Reidy, Keith Warrington

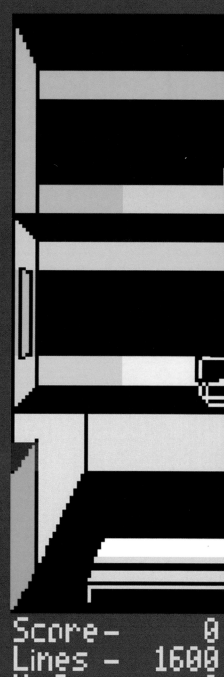

Graphics alone do not make a game, but jaws did hit the floor back in 1985 when *Fairlight's* astounding visuals were seen by the gaming public and journalists alike - its beauty alone was enough for many to purchase the game. The author of *Fairlight*, Jo Jangeborg, hit the headlines the previous year with his graphical package called '*The Artist*'. Jangeborg confesses to using much of its code to create the graphical engine that runs the world in *Fairlight*, a program he called GRAX. The game pushes the Spectrum to its technical limits and on many an occasion GRAX groans under the strain of producing such detailed rooms to explore - if you listen closely, the absence of sound is deafening; if you look closely you will notice 'black' screens between each location as the engine struggles to draw and push the location onto the screen. *Fairlight* was, and still is, the game you load to impress your mum – a wonderful aesthetically pleasing game, with a great adventure interwoven into the graphics engine to boot.

Name	:	Commando
Year	:	1985
Publisher	:	Elite Systems Ltd
Author	:	Keith Burkhill, Nigel Alderton, Rory C. Green, Karen Trueman

A quintessentially British game in every respect, the original *Skool Daze* beautifully captured the disenchanted childhood of Spectrum gamers born into the crumbling world of Thatcherite dominion. Its sequel, **Back to Skool**, built on these rock solid foundations while expanding the world of its delinquent main character, Eric. After successfully pilfering his report card in *Skool Daze*, Eric is charged with sneaking it back into the headmaster's safe before his perfect crime is discovered. A beautifully constructed farce ensues that takes Eric through every room in the institution, and even out of the door to the girl's school next door to recruit nefarious assistance from his fetching girlfriend Haley; and all this while still getting in a full day of school (or, at least, not getting caught for legging it). Although *Skool Daze* set the standard, it was *Back to Skool* that really fulfilled on the promise of a hilarious and invigorating adventure that we were more than happy to skive school, in order to play over and over again.

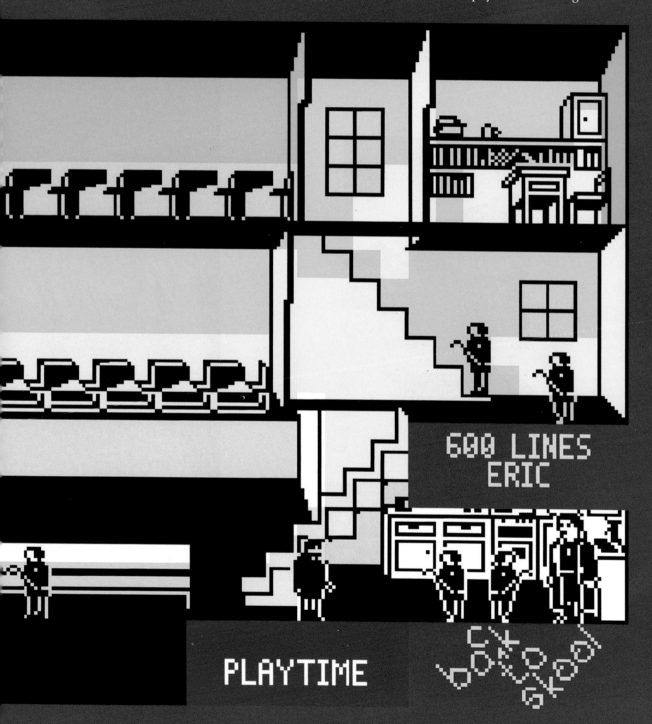

600 LINES
ERIC

PLAYTIME

Name	:	Nodes of Yesod
Year	:	1985
Publisher	:	Odin Computer Graphics
Author	:	Steve Wetherill, Colin Grunes, Stuart James Fotheringham, Paul Salmon, Fred Gray

Charlemagne Fotheringham-Grunes is hearing strange signals coming from the moon and decides to go and investigate. So he grabs his space helmet and catches the number 73 Space Shuttle to the cheesy planet where he meets up with his mate Lunar Mole. Together they explore the moon's surface in search of eight crystal keys. Now Neil Armstrong on his visit back in '69 never mentioned bumping into such creatures as teddy bears on springs, mechanical tortoises or worse still, space muggers who relieve him of any crystals he may have collected. Well that is the challenge Charlemagne faces, as you guide him through the huge number of locations, help him avoid the local inhabitants and solve the many, not so taxing, puzzles that frequently pop up. The graphical style of the game has to be commended as well as the somersaulting animation of the main adventurer. This is also another one of those games that uses sampled speech here and there in the game and the 128K version sports a cracking tune.

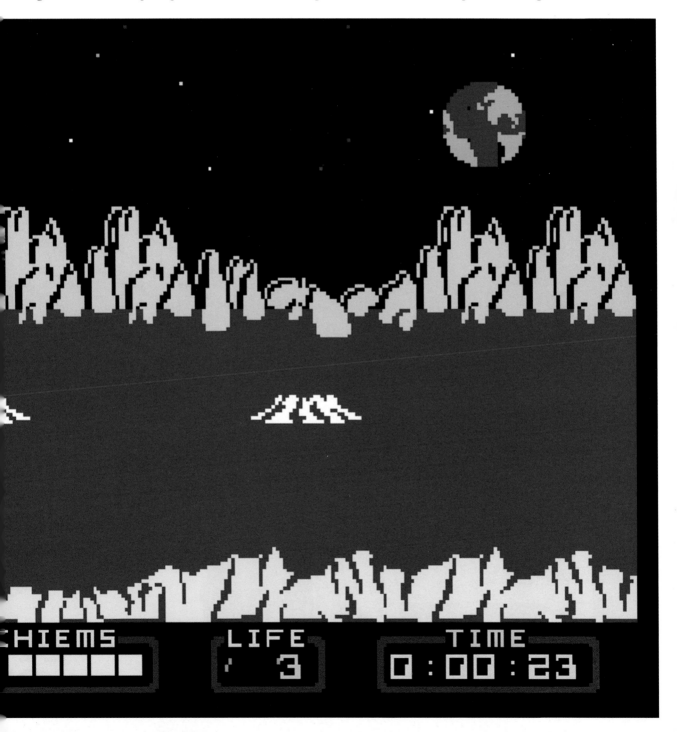

Name	:	Fairlight
Year	:	1985
Publisher	:	The Edge
Author	:	Bo Jangeborg, Jack Wilkes, Niclas Osterlin, Pennsoft, Mark Alexander

48K Spectrum

No, this wasn't based on the 1985 Arnie flick of the same name, although you'd be forgiven for tying the two together given the similarity of their premise. Indeed, this game is likely inspired more by Rambo: First Blood, which had a massive cultural impact on the early 80s. *Commando* was one of the first gaming experiences that delivered on Hollywood's brand of shoot-first-ask-questions-never, grenade toting, boots first, balls out, Commie killing, jungle trashing, shootin'-from-the-hip action spectaculars. That said, *Commando* was also closely related to the scrolling vertical shoot-'em-up genre that was so prolific at the time. It also saw players making their way interminably up-screen, shooting anything and everything that crossed their paths. The difference being that scrolling was, to a degree, under player control, and that was a transformative mechanic that made the game into such a delightful, bullet-soaked romp. Simple enough in the arcades that the Spectrum was able to handle the conversion effortlessly, this was the go-to game for any Spec-chums who needed to vent a little pent up steam.

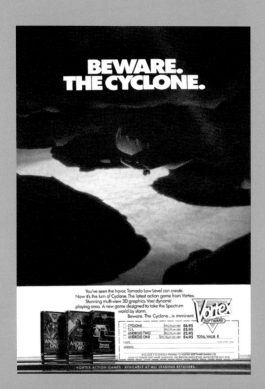

Name   :   Cyclone
Year   :   1985
Publisher   :   Vortex Software
Author   :   Costa Panayi

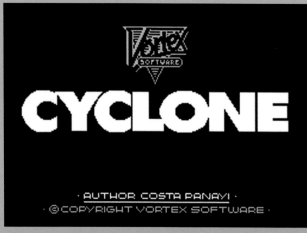

Cyclone is visually similar to its stable partner, *T.L.L.* - it's the same game engine with the Tornado swapped out for a Sea King Helicopter and the gameplay tweaked accordingly for the behaviour of the rotary bladed machine. Tension is the name of the game here as a swirling cyclone is sweeping the land causing windy destruction in its path and intent on downing airborne craft. Your quest is to navigate the many islands on your map in order to rescue the pixelated inhabitants, collect cargo and fuel and avoid the cyclone at all costs – if it gets too close then control of your helicopter is compromised and at worst, you plummet to the ground and break into bits. *Cyclone* is a handsome game with a 3D engine that shows off the best the Spectrum has to offer. The game is a slower affair than *T.L.L.* but this is not a bad thing - the intense panic the game instils when you feel the control in your helicopter slip through your fingers literally makes your heart skip a beat.

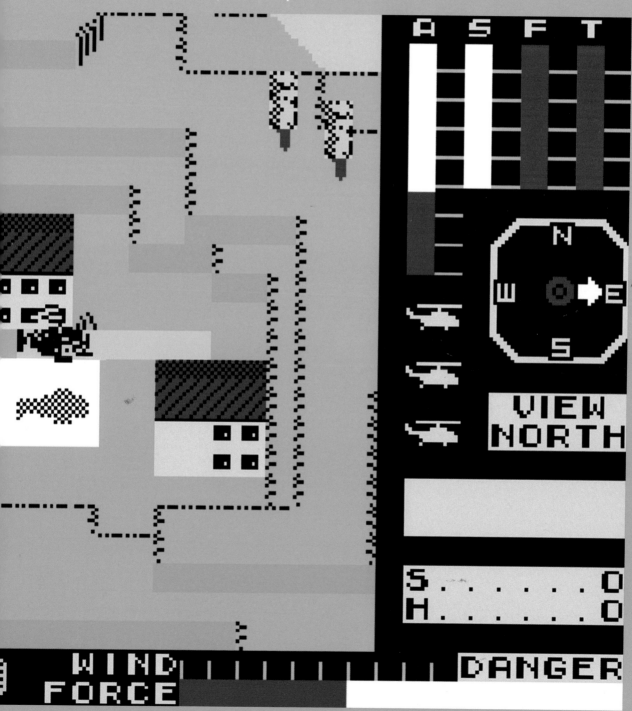

DURELL

Name	:	Saboteur
Year	:	1985
Publisher	:	Durell
Author	:	Clive Townsend

L ots of games drew upon the excitement, mystery and violence that surrounded martial arts in the entertainment media, and *Saboteur* can be counted firmly among them. What it did differently was to offer other aspects of the virtual ninja by including stealth gameplay and espionage themes. Taking on the role of the eponymous, nameless saboteur, players were tasked with silently infiltrating an enemy's lair to retrieve some sensitive floppy disks. Back then, floppy disks were pretty cutting edge, you understand; in other ninja-themed escapades they'd still have been stealing manila folders. Anyway, the journey through this dangerous world relied as much on exploration, quick reflexes and carefully choosing your fights, although there was also a healthy dose of high kicking, shurikens and neck-breaking, natch. Security systems were in place that had to be avoided or defeated, and enemies would set out after you if you made too much noise. *Saboteur* set the standard for deeper, richer martial arts games and still provides lashings of inspiration for its spiritual successors.

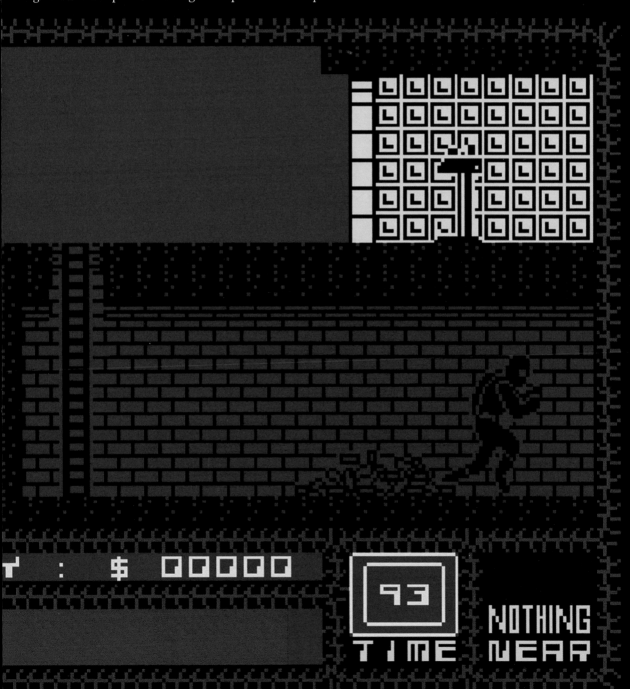

Name	:	Hyper Sports
Year	:	1985
Publisher	:	Imagine
Author	:	Jonathan M. Smith

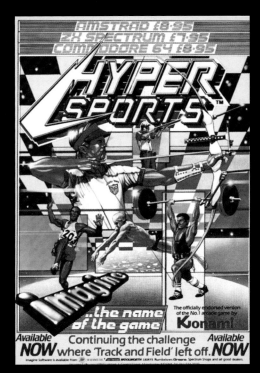

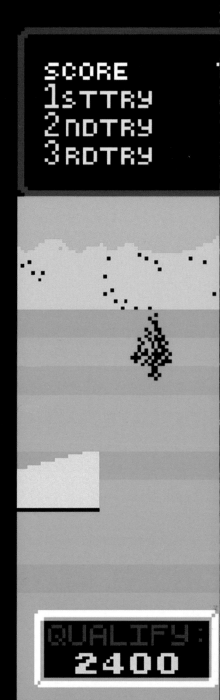

Hyper Sports plays a similar game to *Daley Thompsons Decathlon* but does so with a cheeky wink and a comedic stride. The same joystick waggle gets your moustached 70's athlete trundling down the swim lane, or down the running track but there are a variety of events in *Hyper Sports* that require a little more strategy and timing over Daley and doing well in them is extremely satisfying. Take the archery for example – timing your shot and getting the angle just right is rewarded with the 'NICE' speech bubble that just makes you glow inside, followed by your athlete jumping up and down with glee as he celebrates your success. And this is the same story with each event; be it swimming, triple jump, horse or skeet shooting – each is exhilarating. This is a game completely created by Jonathan Smith and the quality in each event just oozes the 'Joffa' charm and technical wizardry. *Hyper Sports*, based on the Konami original arcade game, is the best of class on the ZX Spectrum and nothing in this genre of game thereafter came close.

0   START GAME

1   KEYBOARD

2   AGF + PROTEK

3   KEMPSTON + I2L

4   INTERFACE 2

Name	:	Spy Hunter
Year	:	1985
Publisher	:	U.S. Gold
Author	:	Denton Designs, F. David Thorpe

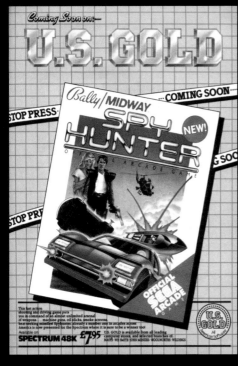

SCOR
000052

Spy Hunter is another colossus arcade sensation, ported onto the humble 8-bit Spectrum – this time by Denton Designs and published through US Gold. The Bally Midway game is a road-race-cum-river racer that resembles very much an old school vertical shooter. There are effectively two sections to the game – the first finds you on the highway where you can select your weapon from the aptly named 'Weapons Van'. You then guide your car on a torturous scrolling, winding road dodging cars, vans and bikes that look like they have come straight off the set of a Bond movie. Veer off the road down a side road and your car turns into a speedboat and the chase continues on the water. *Spy Hunter* is a thrilling race 'n' chase game that just keeps going and going, allowing you to rack up the points by ramming the enemy vehicles into the scenery - or just shooting them down as you would in *Space Invaders*. It has to be said, the scrolling graphics on this port are some of the best you will see on the ZX Spectrum.

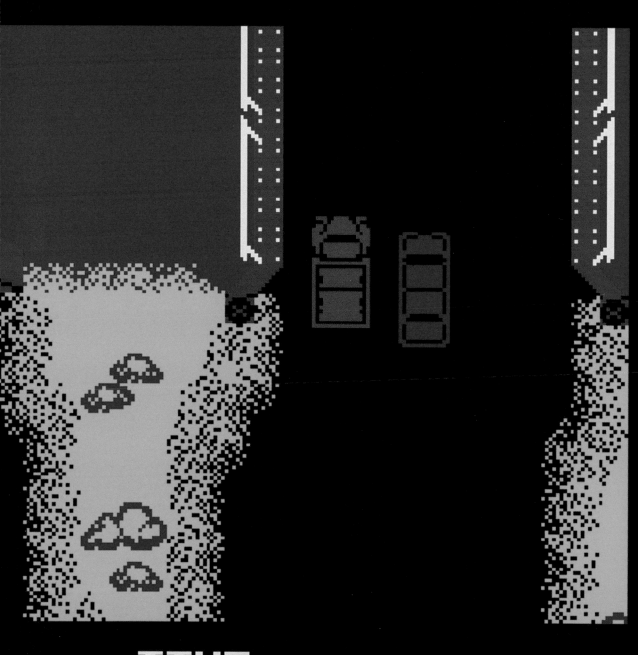

TIME
545

Name	:	Spellbound
Year	:	1985
Publisher	:	Masteronic Added Dimension
Author	:	David Jones, Rob Hubbard, Ray Owen

A t exactly the same time as David Jones created the revolutionary (really) Windimation control system, Gimbal the Wizard cocked up his rice pudding spell and transported Magic Knight and several characters from time and space into a crazy, puzzle-laden castle (complete with delightful roof garden). And so began this deeply addictive graphical adventure/platformer. The premise is easy - find the objects, use them in the right room, give them to the right character, cast the right spells, rescue Gimbal and put everyone back in their place in the universe - simple. The puzzles required some serious thinking (and luck), and even then you still needed to find out where Florin the Dwarf or Samsun the Strong had wandered off to. In a world where 'save game' wasn't an option, this would consume hours and days and months. Reload the tape, restart the game, get stuck, give up for the day, repeat. Until eventually, Your Sinclair provided the solution (yes, yes, cheating). Beautiful, creative, frustrating and ingenious and all of this for £2.99. We had it good in 1985.

Colin Anderton

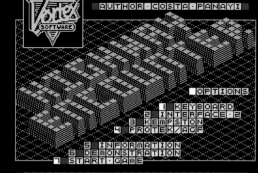

Name	:	Highway Encounter
Year	:	1985
Publisher	:	Vortex Software
Author	:	Costa Panayi

PREPARE YOURSELF FOR THE HIGHWAY ENCOUNTER.

M any a Dr. Who fan were thrilled to play *Highway Encounter*, as they took control of what looked very much like a Dalek – a Dalek whose sole purpose was to literally 'sweep', council style, the road ahead. Parked at the end of the dual carriageway strip is the mother ship of a bunch of aliens that have invaded Earth. Your quest is to lead a team of 'Vorton' buddies as they push along Pandora's box down mile after mile of tarmacked road until it's introduced to the craft. Along the way you have to zip around shooting baddies and try to keep a nice clear path for your not so intelligent space-bin friends to move along on. Thirty zones later and the little box of doom trundles along to the mother ship and unleashes the laser from hell on its hull. The ship goes 'ploop' as it's destroyed and the game ends – taunting you to have another go. *Highway Encounter* is a simple, original and good looking game that has been executed with sheer Vortex class.

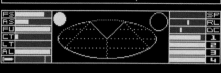

Name	:	Elite
Year	:	1985
Publisher	:	Firebird Software
Author	:	Philip Mochan, Ricardo J.M. Pinto,
		Dominic M.N. Prior, Mark Wighton

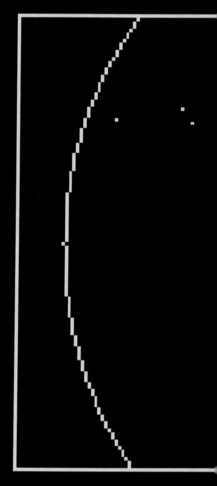

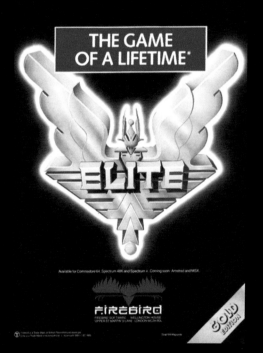

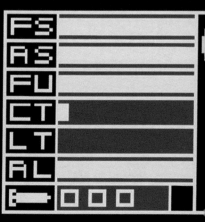

It has to be a sign of *Elite's* innovation that even today, it beggars belief that a universe of this size was miraculously packed into 48KB. It's a feat of engineering that's rarely, if ever, been bested in the gaming world. Setting out into the unreachable blackness of outer space in your trusty Cobra Mk III, with your eyes on the goal of becoming the most feared and respected mercenary in the galaxy. But as the game unfolded and you worked your way up the ranks *Elite* revealed itself to harbour far greater depth than merely killing other space farers. A complex trading system allowed you to make necessary upgrades to your ship, where local economies affected the price of different goods, weapons, parts and supplies. And considering the sheer volume of planets and space stations populating the universe of *Elite*, success demanded as much intelligence as it did brawn. That's why *Elite* is still remembered as the thinking man's game, and not just another digital dog fight.

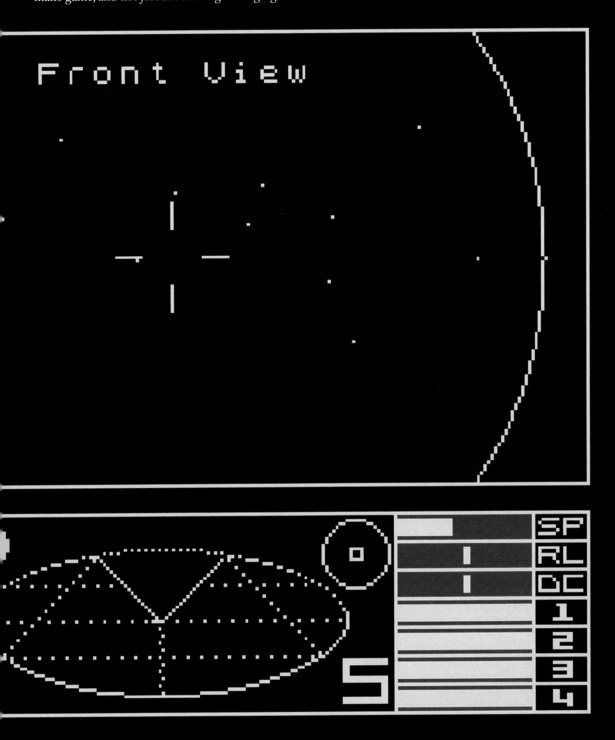

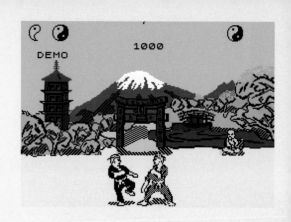

Melbourne House

Name	:	The Way of the Exploding Fist
Year	:	1985
Publisher	:	Melbourne House
Author	:	Gregg Barnett, Greg Holland, Steven Taylor, William Tang

Coin-op classic *Karate Champ* never really made it into the living rooms of the 1980s gamer, but it's not like we were starved of one-on-one tournament fighter options. *The Way of the Exploding Fist*, by way of a very fine example. Bouts were against another player, or the CPU, pitting you toe-to-toe against increasingly skilful fighters as you worked toward the much-lauded 10th Dan rank. Moves were numerous, requiring precise joystick and button combinations to pull off devastating attacks, and game-changing defences. Accurate hit-detection, smashing visuals and bone-crunching audio conspired to make *Exploding Fist* stand out among its many peers. Button mashing is a relatively new invention, which didn't work one bit in the days of the *Exploding Fist*, we're very happy to say. Fighting games like this demanded skill and dedication to master, much like the martial art disciplines they were simulating, bringing the characters closer to real life combatants than many of your new fangled console titles are able to achieve.

Name	:	Rebelstar
Year	:	1986
Publisher	:	Firebird Software
Author	:	Julian Gollop, Simon Clarke

Sometimes overlooked in the Julian Gollop canon, stuck as it is between the simple ingenious purity of *Chaos* and the epic space adventure of *Laser Squad*, 1986 turn-based game *Rebelstar* is a fascinating snapshot of a genre – and a developer – in transition. As the Rebelstar Raiders, the aim of this £1.99 gem was to break into a secure bunker and shut down the malfunctioning AI that had stolen your secret plans. As plots go, it's hardly original, but where mechanics are concerned *Rebelstar* represented a huge leap forwards for strategy gaming. The world itself was far more interactive than anything previous, allowing debris to block doors and passages and objects to be picked up and dropped. Suddenly, planning your next advance and reacting to unscripted changes to the map became imperative. Even the combat felt fresh with features such as 'opportunity fire' which allowed inactive units to attack enemies that passed through their field of vision. A basic trick, perhaps, but one that made *Rebelstar's* sci-fi grunts feel like actual soldiers with battlefield smarts, not just chess pieces waiting to be taken.

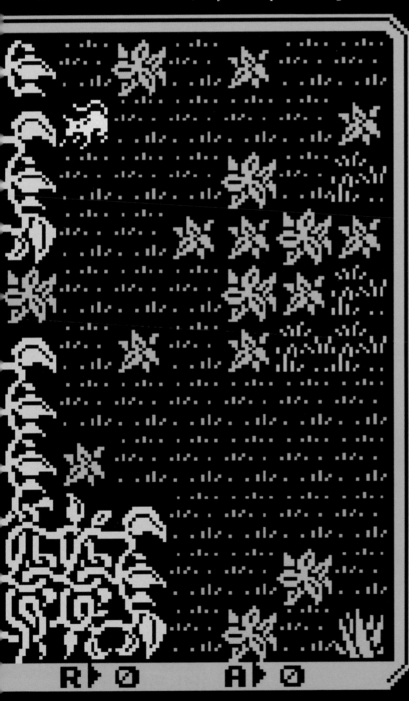

MARSH
RAT
MORALE▶
NERVOUS
STAMINA▶
GREAT
ACTION
POINTS▶
19
PROTEC▶
0

K=CANCEL
I=INFO
F=FIRE
  MODE
M=DROP
  OBJECT
O=CHANGE
  OBJECT
P=PICKUP
  OBJECT
L=LOAD

R▶0   A▶0

Name	:	Roller Coaster
Year	:	1986
Publisher	:	Elite Systems
Author	:	S. Brockelhurst

As a youngster, going to the fair was a treat - there was always so much to do including playing all the latest arcade machines. *Roller Coaster* taps into the sounds and sights of a typical theme park as you take control of the old Colonel as he explores his land of pleasure, collecting up the money bags strewn in and around the many rides and stalls that are typical of this kind of establishment. *Roller Coaster* is a platformer at heart and the many ways of losing one of your limited lives in the game are quite unique – being hit by a dodgem, frazzled on the electric lines of the roller coaster or even drowning in the water of the log flume are some of the imaginative ways of meeting your maker. As you explore the massive sixty screens of the game all your favourites attractions are visited, including the Big Dipper that sweeps you across a number of screens in the park, allowing you to collect swag on the way. Playing *Roller Coaster* is like revisiting Coney Island as an eight year old – you find yourself playing with a big grin on your face.

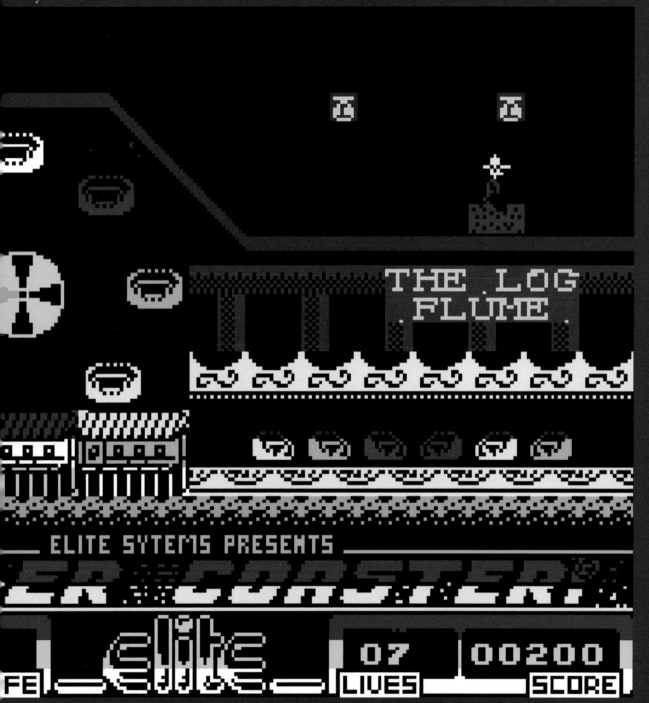

Name	:	The Trap Door
Year	:	1986
Publisher	:	Piranha
Author	:	Don Priestley

MONSTER MANIA

Cans of worms, boiled slimies, and eyeball crush are just some of the delicacies demanded by bumbling Berk's bellowing boss. Can you satisfy the hunger of 'him upstairs' and survive the nasties that come out of the Trap Door? There's always something lurking in the dark waiting to emerge in this hilarious graphic adventure.

· SPECTRUM · COMMODORE · AMSTRAD · £7.95

Available from your local stockist or, in case of difficulty, direct from John Darvill, Macmillan Distribution Ltd, Houndmills, Basingstoke RG21 2XS. Make cheques or postal orders payable to Macmillan Limited and state the machine version you want. Further information on PIRANHA games from:

Richard Bason, Piranha
4 Little Essex Street, London WC2R 3LF
Tel: 01-836 6633

The Trap Door was a quintessentially British 80s kids' TV show. Back then, you could get away with almost anything so long as you avoided sex references (well, kept them to a minimum). This show, voiced by the comedic mastermind Willie Rushton managed to blend dark fantasy and horror with child-friendly humour and its official Spectrum game tie-in was equally masterful. Big, bold characters, the likes of which were rarely seen on the rubber-keyed maestro, took centre stage as players shepherded Berk and Drutt around the castle in an effort to rescue their friend Boni from the catacombs beneath the eponymous cellar trap door. Both Berk and Drutt offered their own unique abilities and switching between them to solve the various puzzles and obstacles strewn about the colourful, yet impressively ominous castle environment made up the core of the game. But this digitised spin-off game oozed thickly with the same sweetly, horror-tinged humour that made *The Trap Door* the cult favourite that it remains today.

Name : Uridium

Year : 1986

Publisher : Hewson Consultants

Author : Dominic Robinson, Stephen J. Crow

There was talk going around the school playground regarding a new arcade game released for the Commodore 64 – this was the next game to get if you owned the beige competitor. The chatter turned some weeks later to the possibility of a Spectrum version – could it really be done? The C64 fans thought not. Dominic Robinson went down in gaming history for his Spectrum conversion of *Uridium* and arguably created a game that is as good, if not better, that it's brethren. A smooth, sideways scrolling arcade romp that sees you attempting to fly your ship to the landing strip at the end of the level, dodging land based objects, waves of alien ships and the arsenal they fire at you as you go. Once you kill enough baddies, the runway opens for business allowing you to park your ship. It's then onto the next level where there are new objects to dodge, new aliens to shoot and a world that has magically morphed from a shade of blue to a shade of green. Until the arrival of R-Type some years later, *Uridium* was the king of scrolling shoot-em-ups.

MIKRO-GEN

THREE 'WEEKS' IN
PARADISE!

MIKRO-GEN '86

DON'T
FEED THE
ANIMALS

SPECIAL
KEYS:
 3: TURN WALLY'S COLOUR ON/OFF.
 4: PAUSE THE GAME.
 5: TURN TUNE IN GAME ON/OFF.

Name	:	Three Weeks in Paradise
Year	:	1986
Publisher	:	Mikro-Gen Ltd
Author	:	David Perry, Nick Jones, Neil Strudwick

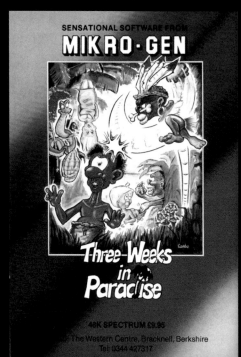

SENSATIONAL SOFTWARE FROM
MIKRO·GEN

Three Weeks
in
Paradise

48K SPECTRUM £9.95
The Western Centre, Bracknell, Berkshire
Tel: 0344 427317

NOTHIN

NOTHIN

THREE WEEKS
IN PARADISE

MIKRO·GEN

This would be Wally Week's swan song as he retired from the gaming scene forever, but he did it in superb style. Developer Mikro-Gen beautifully aped the growing trend for British holidaymakers to descend on some quaint European resort and set about turning it into Blackpool without the rain. But Wally gets a holiday he wasn't expecting. The locals (read natives) have snatched his family and plan on turning them into a hearty meal. So you once again step up as Wally and embark on a hilarious adventure to prevent you and your kinfolk from becoming lunch. The average Speccy gamer was growing up, and Mikro-Gen understood this. Humour needed to be more salacious, and cut a fraction closer to the bone (sorry Wally; bad choice of words), and that's just what *Three Weeks in Paradise* delivered. Wally Week deserves greater recognition as a games mascot than he's ever likely to receive. He turned the ordinary blue collar Brit into a hero, and we'll always remember him fondly thanks to his grand 8-bit adventures.

Name	:	Bomb Jack
Year	:	1986
Publisher	:	Elite Systems Ltd
Author	:	Paul Holmes, Andy Williams, Karen Trueman

Even in 1984 when *Bomb Jack* was originally brought into the arcades, there weren't many game designers coming out with particularly original ideas. Either because it was considered too risky to be overly original, or because they simply couldn't think of new ways to coax 10p from our pockets. But *Bomb Jack* can't easily be accused of copying anything that came before it, and it migrated to the home systems beautifully. Some dastardly deviant has been placing bombs at famous locations around the world, and only superhero Bomb Jack can come to the rescue. He's a quirky chap with unique powers. While he can't exactly fly, what he can do is leap high in a very controlled manner, and then glide around as he descends. This still equips him to snaffle up the irksome explosives. Once the first has been collected, a detonation sequence is activated and Jack must get to each lit bomb in turn as quickly as possible. It was a colourful and detailed rendition on the Spectrum that did the spunky superhero proud.

Name	:	Bobby Bearing
Year	:	1986
Publisher	:	The Edge
Author	:	Robert Figgins, Trevor Figgins

An unconvincing storyline does not necessarily a bad game make – *Bobby Bearing* is a metallic robotic ball wossname and his cousin (?) has led his brother balls astray on to the plains of a 'monochrome' world. Bob has to rescue them before it's too late. Harrowing stuff. Thankfully the game does not need a great storyline to be the good game it is. In his search, Bobby has to roll around an isometric 3D maze-like realm adhering to the rules of inertia – travel at the right speed and slopes can be climbed, travelling a little too slowly and it's back down the slope he goes. Death in the game is impossible – when the counter hits 0 and your family are nowhere to be seen it is 'Game Over'. Obstacles in Bobby's way continually try to slow him down – malicious fangled spheres will steer him off course and moving blocks are keen to flatten him to a pulp, taking valuable seconds off the clock. A therapeutic, absorbing game where it's just as relaxing rolling and bouncing around the screens – finding your brothers is just a bonus.

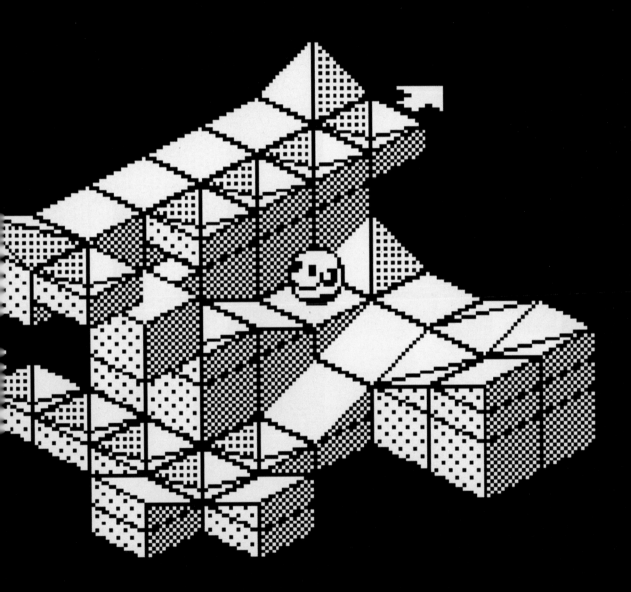

BARNABY

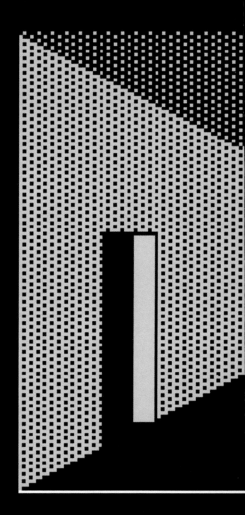

Name	:	Jack The Nipper
Year	:	1986
Publisher	:	Gremlin Graphics
Author	:	Greg A. Holmes, Nick Laa, Peter M. Harrap, John Holmes

With age comes some degree of responsibility – with *Jack the Nipper* the rules go out of the window as you are encouraged to go back to being an 'innocent' infant and with the look of 'Who me?' on your cherub face, be as naughty as possible. *Jack the Nipper* has a glorious comic book graphical style as you go about being naughty scaring cats, putting glue on dentures, blowing up police stations and carrying out many more 'Dennis the Menace' type japes that all contribute to Jack filling up his 'naughtyometer' to the magical hundred per cent. Of course if you get caught then a spanking is in order that inevitably gives Jack nappy rash – something that, if you can remember that far back, is not pleasant and should be avoided. If the rash factor goes critical one of Jack's young lives is lost. Weep. Lose all your lives and Jack parades onto the screen with sarcastic tone. If you're feeling a little naughty tonight, then why not load this game up for a quick blast.

AGENT X GAME SELECTION

1 START GAME

2 KEYBOARD CONTROL
3 KEMPSTON JOYSTICK
4 CURSOR JOYSTICK
5 SINCLAIR JOYSTICK

(C)1986 Program by Steven Tatlock
Graphics by John Tatlock
5 Channel music by Tim Follin

Name	:	Agent X
Year	:	1986
Publisher	:	Mastertronic
Author	:	Steven Tatlock, John P. Tatlock,
		Tim Follin

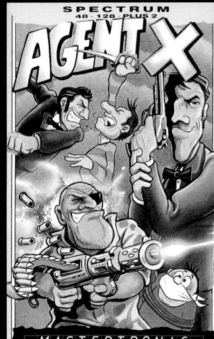

A gent X is a good game, don't get me wrong, but the most memorable part for many is the musical score that comes out of the Spectrum's mono speaker once the game has loaded. It is written by Tim Follin and boasts five channels – which considering that the beeper sound chip in the machine is just the one, is quite a claim. But when you listen to it you cannot quite believe what you're hearing. For £1.99 on the Mastertronic budget label you get quite a lot of bang for your buck with *Agent X* with four sections that have to be played in order to save a kidnapped President. Playing the part of an undercover spy sees you drive your spy-mobile through busy traffic; kick and fight your way through a swarm of enemies; practice your target shooting, then negotiate a helicopter through a cavernous complex in search of a bomb which is then used to kill the mad scientist kidnapper. *Agent X* is a great game due to the sum of its parts – 4 average unique game sections and a great tune.

Name	:	Wizball
Year	:	1987
Publisher	:	Ocean Software
Author	:	Steven L. Watson, Mark R. Jones,
		Peter Clarke, Paul Owens

PL1 000000

I the title marked 'They Don't Make 'Em Like This Any More', Sensible Software's *Wizball* is surely near the top of the pile. Part horizontal shoot-em-up, part exploration game, part colouring-in simulator, the game is a genuinely unique proposition the likes of which had never been seen before – or have been seen since. Cast as a wizard who has transformed into a hovering ball, and accompanied by his feline 'catellite', your task is to restore colour to the world by shooting enemies and collecting the drips of paint that fall from them. That the Speccy and its famous colour issues managed to replicate this C64 original is a testament to the Ocean staff's coding skills. It's a tough game too, starting you with incredibly limited movement as you bounce around and forcing you to earn tokens that will unlock the abilities needed to not only complete the game, but navigate its stages with anything resembling accuracy. Sensible Software is probably best known today for its eponymous 16-bit soccer game, but it's the surreal 8-bit *Wizball* that typified the company's leftfield genius.

HI 100000

Name	:	Head Over Heels
Year	:	1987
Publisher	:	Ocean Software
Author	:	Jon Ritman, Bernie Drummond,
		F. David Thorpe, Guy Stevens

While *Knight Lore* was the game that most people remember as the king of the isometric adventure on the Spectrum, for me it's perhaps the less well-known *Head Over Heels* that holds a special place in my heart. Released in 1987 and published by Ocean Software, the game was made by Jon Ritman and Bernie Drummond, who were personal heroes of mine during the Spectrum era, having created the wonderful *Batman* and *Match Day* titles. The concept was groundbreaking; you controlled two characters, each with very different individual abilities (Heels was fast, but couldn't jump, Head could jump but was slow) but you could also combine them letting you use their abilities together in a complementary way. It was a crazy big game, with more than 300 screens requiring a combination of good reflexes for avoiding bad guys, as well as puzzle solving, memory and mapmaking. The game was extremely influential on me and throughout my own career as a video-game developer I've strived to include those key elements of co-operation and diverse gameplay wherever I can.

Paul Weaver

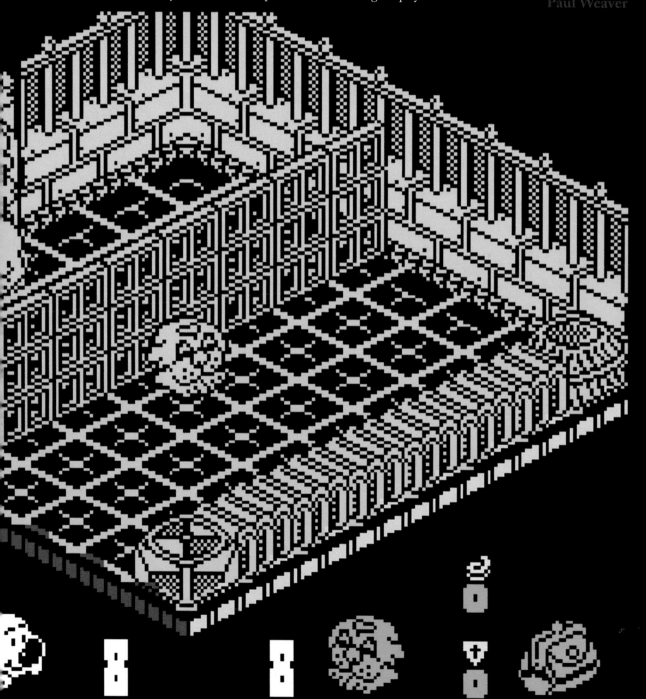

B U B B L E   B O B B L E

CHOOSE CONTROL FOR PLAYER 1

1. KEYBOARD
2. SINCLAIR
3. KEMPSTON
4. CURSOR TYPE

LICENSED BY FIREBIRD SOFTWARE

Name	:	Bubble Bobble
Year	:	1987
Publisher	:	Firebird Software
Author	:	Mike Follin, Andrew R. Threlfall, Tim Follin

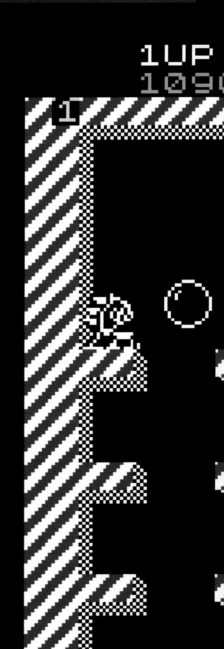

Two player games weren't exactly common on the Spectrum, but neither could they be easily classed as rare. Co-operative two player games, on the other hand, were - and *Bubble Bobble* was one of the finest examples as to why playing together was better than playing against each other. Cute and crazy, as only the Japanese know how, the game features Bub and Bob; two bubble blowing dragons who jump around single-screen levels, capturing a wild variety of weird creatures inside their mouth-blown bubbles. Players had to be quick on their claws to pop these bubbles before the creatures escaped, and clear the level within a tight time limit. A host of power-ups and special items appeared on the screen offering such strange delights as fast bubbles, extra bubble-blowing distance, a faster dragon, fireballs, time freezing and jumping ahead through multiple levels. Despite the similarity of each level, playing *Bubble Bobble* was somehow never boring, and the quality of its Spectrum adaptation proved the rubber keyed warrior's prowess.

 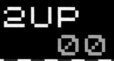

Name	:	Flying Shark
Year	:	1987
Publisher	:	Firebird Software
Author	:	Dominic Robinson, John Cumming, Gavin Wade, Drew Northcott

HOT FROM THE ARCADES, FLYING SHARK IS
THE ULTIMATE SHOOT-EM-UP FROM TAITO.
BOMB AND BLAST YOUR WAY INTO
ARCADE HISTORY.

Spectrum £7.95 Commodore & Amstrad £8.95 (£12.95 & £14.95 d) Atari ST £19.95

PLAYER ONE 1UP

2000

Gaming was maturing very quickly toward the back end of the 80s as strategic and management games proved just how in-depth, profound and engaging digital experiences could be. But sometimes we just wanted to blow stuff up. At times like that we turned to the arcades, where it was all about instant gratification and bullet-riddled death. *Flying Shark* brought that glorious destruction home as you took to the skies in a heavily-armed biplane to bring down an entire army of advancing military machines. This was the epitome of vertically scrolling shooters, taking you on adventures over land and sea with nothing to worry about other than dodging bullets, missiles and bombs while delivering fast and brutal retribution to anything that moved. It's not a game that inspired thought or consideration. It was gratuitous relief, which was the reason we all started playing computer games in the first place. Raining fire on random enemies is what *Flying Shark* was all about and reminds us that there'll always be a place for mindless death and destruction in the video games world.

Name	:	Match Day 2
Year	:	1987
Publisher	:	Ocean Software
Author	:	Jon Ritman, Bernie Drummond, Guy Stevens, Ivan Horn

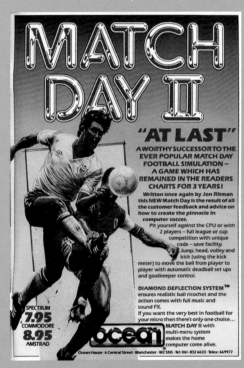

RITMAN

Match Day II quickly established itself as one of the best digital football games the Spectrum ever saw; and the competition in this genre was extremely tough. To cut down on processor strain and to declutter the field a little, the number of players on each team was reduced to seven. But this had the required effect and made *Match Day II* immeasurably playable. A very fair trade off between realism and playability that a lot of games could still learn from. It was also one of the first footy games that delivered complete control over the ball. You didn't just kick it in the direction you were facing. *Match Day II* provided realistic rebound effects when the ball struck a player, and allowed you to precisely control the power behind a shot, or a pass. You didn't have to actually like football to enjoy this game, as it was every bit a stunning computer game as it was a sports simulation. The players even had realistic 70s Kevin Keegan-style perms. What's not to love about that?

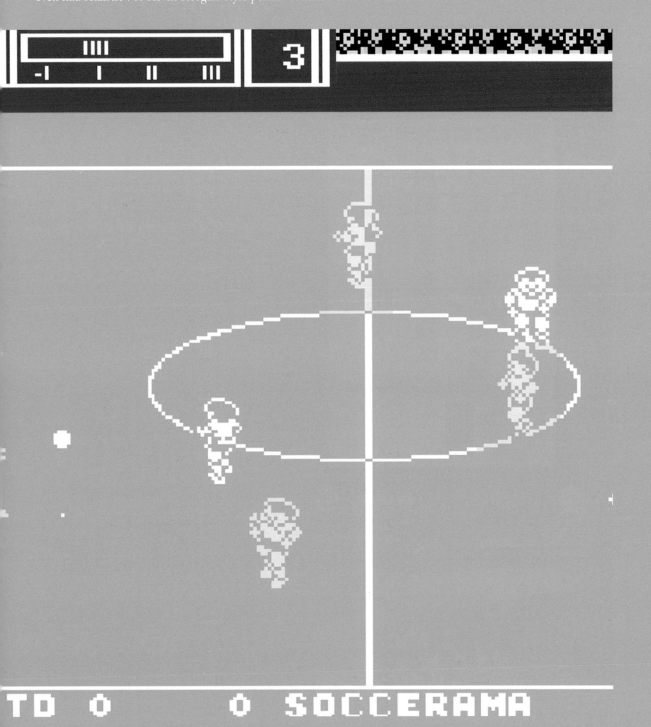

THE FUN STARTS HERE

Name	:	Dizzy
Year	:	1987
Publisher	:	Codemasters
Author	:	The Oliver Twins, Jon Paul Eldridge

All the Dizzy games were great. The first one laid (tee-hee) the foundations and, for many, will be the most beloved because it was the inaugural beautiful, explorative adventure in the world of the Yolk Folk. But truth be told, it was the third outing for Dizzy (not counting Fast Food) where he really hit his pace. *Fantasy World Dizzy* significantly expanded the limited view that we'd previously seen of Dizzy and his people introducing us to various other Yolk Folk while balancing the difficulty level to nigh-on perfection, improving the inventory and allowing multiple ways to complete the game. Of course, rescuing his girlfriend Daisy from the clutches of the evil wizard in the cloud castle was the preferred method and showed you the extent of the game's incredible design work. All this was delivered at budget range prices, as was the way for all the Dizzy games, and the sheer addictiveness of its lengthy and elaborate gameplay put the full price titles that *Fantasy World Dizzy* was sharing shelf space with to shame.

Name	:	Auf Wiedersehen Monty
Year	:	1987
Publisher	:	Gremlin Graphics
Author	:	Shaun Hollingworth, Peter M. Harrap, Chris Kerry, Steve Kerry, Colin Dooley, Greg A. Holmes, Terry Lloyd, Ben Daglish

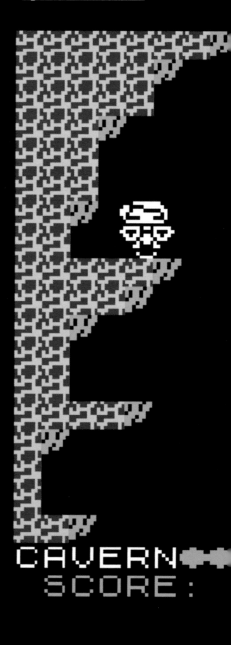

Although it's a long time since he popped his head above ground, Monty was something of an unofficial mascot for the Spectrum. This was his fourth outing, and arguably one of his best. He's out and about looking for somewhere new to live and has opted for the Greek island of Montos. He doesn't just want to live there, of course. Monty's had a busy life in the public eye (of Speccy gamers) and wants to buy the place so he can retire. Collecting the money and goodies required to seal the deal means a platforming adventure across all of Europe and his adventures are rife with the kind of salacious humour and pop culture references Monty was famous for. Indeed, the game's title is just such a reference being named after the excellent British comedy show 'Auf Wiedersehen, Pet' and it pokes fun at the occupants of Europe in just the same way that Oz, Neville, Den, Bomber, Wayne and the gang did on their travels. This would be Monty's final platformer, and was a wonderful way to say goodbye to our favourite mole.

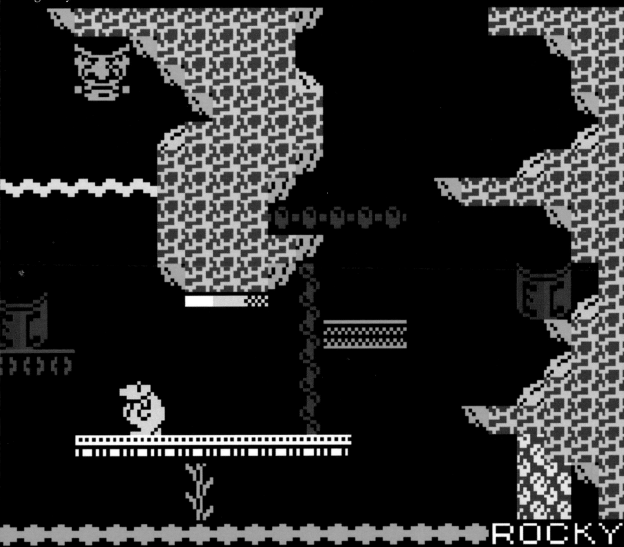

Name	:	The Sentinel
Year	:	1987
Publisher	:	Firebird Software
Author	:	Mike Follin, Geoff Crammond, Tim Follin

Considered by many to be one of the earliest examples of virtual reality gaming, *The Sentinel* took home computers to new realms through its solid-filled 3D graphics, huge number of levels and very unique gameplay. The visuals were simply stunning, but incredibly taxing for computers of the day. To help the noble Speccy cope with the solid polygons of *The Sentinel*, the gameplay essentially fixes you in place. So you can look around the stunningly realistic environments (?!), but the telepathing robot you're in control of can't explore them. Not directly, anyway. What it can do is manipulate objects dotted about the place to build itself another robotic frame, and then transfer its sentient programming to this new host. By working your way through these additional entities you made your way from the lowest regions of the 3D world to the highest peak where *The Sentinel* stands. Absorb it, and the world is yours. But it also required careful management of your energy allocations and that turned out to be a gameplay mechanic that's echoed throughout the industry today.

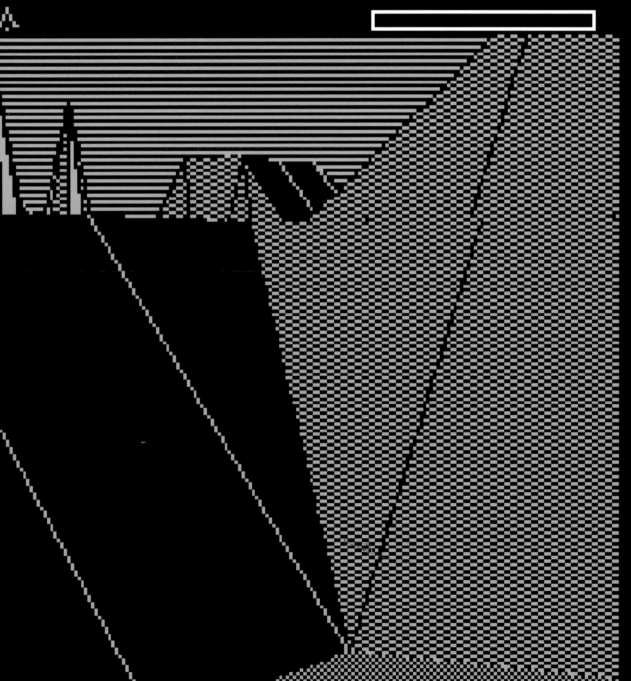

Name : Feud
Year : 1987
Publisher : Bulldog Software
Author : John Pickford, Ste Pickford, Pete
Harrison, David Whittaker

STE A B.D.L PRODUCTION ©1987 BULLDOG

FEUD

FEUD

1 KEYBOARD
2 KEMPSTON JOYSTICK
3 INTERFACE TWO
4 CURSOR JOYSTICK

0 START GAME

© BULLDOG 1987.

SPELL

LEARIC
CONCOC

Players, and more importantly game developers and publishers, were a lot less driven by genre back in the Spectrum's day. It really didn't matter if you were making a shooter, a driving game, a fighter or whatever.

Feud was one of the many games, therefore, that embraced the opportunity to create new and unique types of gameplay and this one is definitely unique. There's only one enemy to defeat but you've only got one day to do it. Your evil twin, who's also a wizard, has cast an ageing spell on you and the only way to break it is to dispatch him. This involves scouring the landscape looking for plants and herbs that you can take back to your base and combine into aggressive and defensive spells. Your twin has exactly the same mission, and is busy mixing his own potions that he can use to kill you or defend against your attacks. It's a superb mechanic being pitted in a game of magical chess against an equal opponent and *Feud* offered massive replay value.

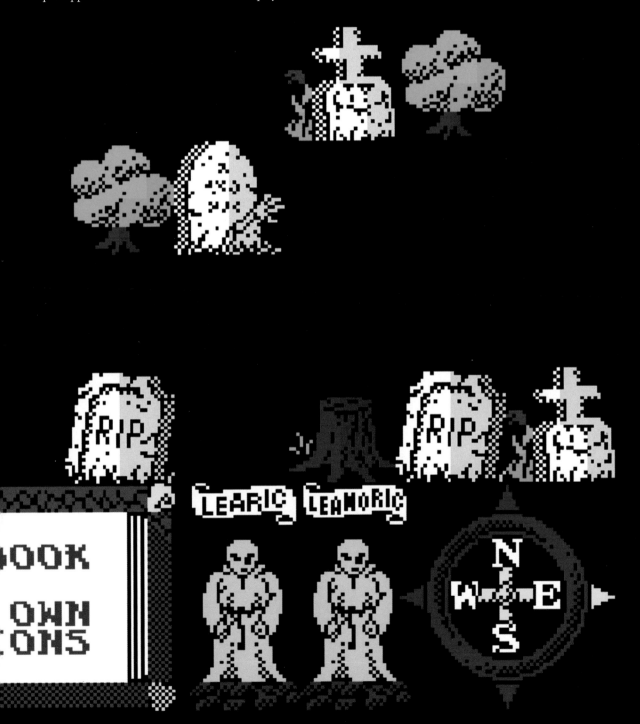

LEVEL : 4

WARRIOR
SCORE HEALTH
1800 1580

PRESS FIRE

Name   :   Gauntlet
Year   :   1987
Publisher :   U.S. Gold
Author   :   Tony R. Porter, Kevin Bulmer, Bill
                 Allen, Ben Daglish

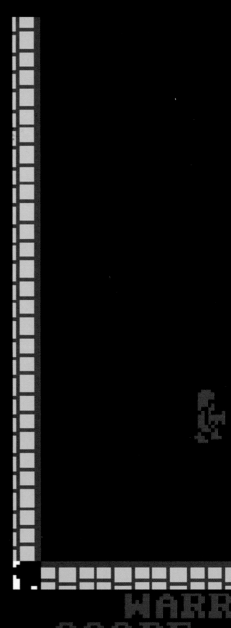

WARR.

SCORE

0

I f there's one thing any adaptation of *Gauntlet* demands, it's the sheer number of enemies in need of thwarting. Running around a dungeon populated by only a handful of ghosts, ghouls and skeletons just wouldn't cut the digital mustard, so you can appreciate the wall that Gremlin Graphics' back was up against in bringing it to the Speccy. *Gauntlet* made gaming history as one of the first ever powerhouse dungeon crawlers which thrilled gamers through its epic armies of enemies beating at the doors and walls to get to your character. Armed with various types of weapons and magic, depending on the role you chose, *Gauntlet* delivered on a host of different genres from hack 'n' slash to RPG and wove them seamlessly together into a fantasy-based roller coaster ride of hot death and action. And the Spectrum conversion was a triumph. Somehow, those 8-bit dungeons were bulging at the seams with legions of supernatural bad guys, such that home computers had never seen.

PRIME DIRECTIVES_

1: SERVE THE PUBLIC TRUST
2: PROTECT THE INNOCENT
3: UPHOLD THE LAW
4: CLASSIFIED_

Name	:	Robocop
Year	:	1988
Publisher	:	Ocean Software
Author	:	Mike Lamb, Dawn Drake, Jonathan Dunn, Bill Harbison

O h my god! The computer just spoke! That was the mind-stopping reaction we all had as, upon loading, the Spectrum's official *RoboCop* game rewarded us with a spoken sample of Murphy's three prime directives. Those short commandments were immediately burned into our gaming consciousness. Ocean's home conversion of Data East's arcade machine was more than just clever sampled speech, however. The cybernetic shoot-'em-up was a stunning effort boasting large detailed visuals that scrolled like they were made of warm butter, while the action delivered on every hyper-violent promise of its Hollywood inspiration. This is one of the rare circumstances where a game actually improved on its long and arduous journey from the arcades to the home platforms, and even today it's easy to appreciate the Spectrum game's superiority over its coin-operated companion. Such was the quality of the Spectrum adaptation that it took over 18 months for another game to topple *Robocop* from the top of the charts, by which time Murphy was the star of one of the Speccy's best selling games of all time.

LOLLY	100000
LOOT	080000
DOSH	060000
BREAD	040000
DOUGH	020000

Name	:	Target: Renegade
Year	:	1988
Publisher	:	Imagine Software
Author	:	Mike Lamb, Dawn Drake, Simon Butler, Jonathan Dunn, Gari Biasillo

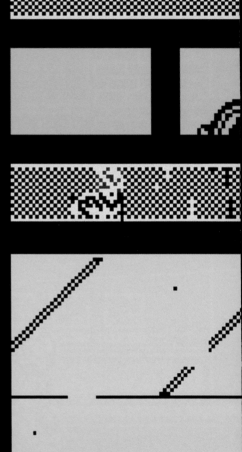

When the long-awaited home conversion of *Double Dragon* completely dropped the ball, Ocean deftly picked it up with its in-house sequel to *Double Dragon's* spiritual predecessor, *Renegade*. The studio was fortunate in that its original *Renegade* license included an option for sequels, which Taito never delivered (not directly, at least). So Ocean made it anyway in the shape of *Target: Renegade,* and put a superbly British spin on the co-operative scrolling beat-'em-up that took players on a two-man rampage through multi-storey car parks, snooker clubs and impoverished ghettos. *Target: Renegade* was a crowning moment in Spectrum gaming history as it proved that Clive's 8-bit warrior was the equal of the arcades. The action was fast, and the fists were furious, as players could finally knock joystick elbows with each other while their nameless characters fought side-by-side on-screen. The co-operative fighting game might not seem so important now but in the Spectrum days it was a revolution, and *Target: Renegade* was leading the charge loud and proud alongside the coin-ops.

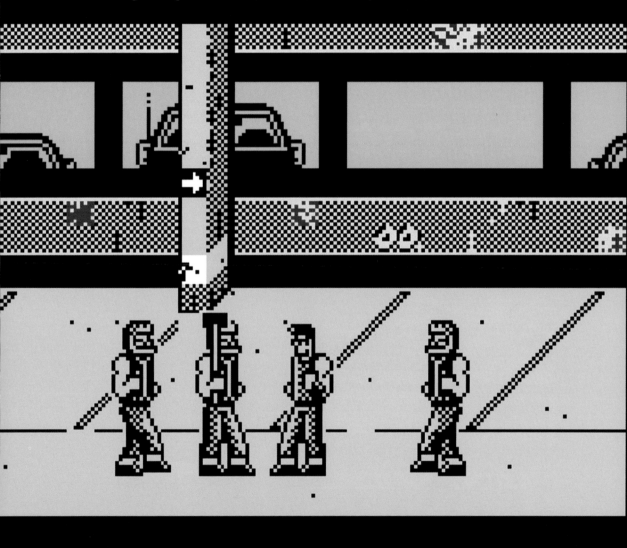

Name	:	R Type
Year	:	1988
Publisher	:	Electric Dreams
Author	:	Bob Pape, Mark A. Jones, Robert L. Hylands

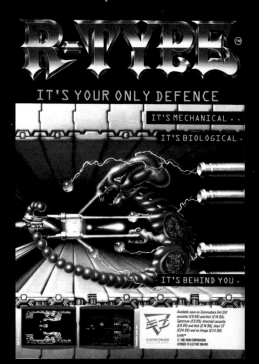

If we ever needed proof that the Speccy was the equal of any other games platform (and we don't) you can find it right here in the home conversion of Irem's spectacular scrolling sci-fi shooter, *R-Type*. You could almost believe that Electric Dreams which handled the conversion found some magical way to break the Spectrum's graphical rules. *R-Type* was the brightest and most colourful game ever to grace the 8-bit beauty, and its gameplay didn't suffer in the slightest due to its luscious, bio-mechanical presentation. To be fair, a major aspect of *R-Type's* gameplay is that it's not a fast-moving fight. That doesn't mean it's any less engaging or action-packed, of course. The introduction of the indestructible Force weapon that could be jettisoned into the crowds of insectoid enemies, and recalled to add extra oomph to your weaponry when reattached proved to be a seminal moment in game design history. *R-Type* is the side-scrolling shooter by which all others are measured, especially on the Spectrum.

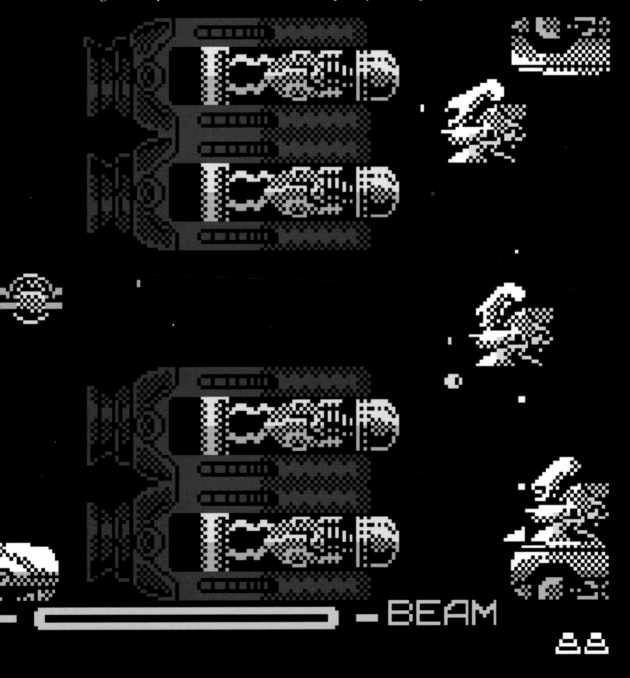

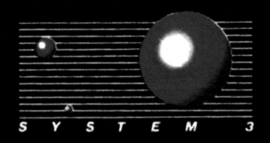

Name	:	Last Ninja 2
Year	:	1988
Publisher	:	System 3
Author	:	Mevlut Dinc, Gary Thornton, Brian Marshall

BASED ON THE AWARD WINNING
INTERNATIONAL BEST SELLERS - LAST NINJA I AND II

SYSTEM 3 SOFTWARE LTD, BLENHEIM HOUSE, 1 ASH HILL DRIVE, PINNER, MIDDLESEX HA5 2AG Tel 081 866 5692 Fax 081 866 8584
AVAILABLE ON SPECTRUM, AMSTRAD CPC, C64, ATARI ST AND AMIGA.

One of the greatest injustices in the history of man is that *The Last Ninja* - one of the most popular and beloved games ever released on another, lesser known home computer called the Compradore 63 (or something) - never made its way to the Spectrum. Fortunately its sequel did, and this was an isometric adventure game of impressive grandeur and scope. Falling through time into the modern day, the ancient assassin continued his (unplayed) quest to bring the evil Shogun Kunitoki to swift and brutal justice on the hard streets of New York, 1988. But the one-time Japanese overlord is now a drug baron, too, and players were suddenly facing futuristic boom-stick weapons as well as deadly shadow warrior techniques. Not that it mattered to a ninja like Armakuni; the deadliest of all martial artists, as firmly established by the B-Movie industry of the 1980s. *Last Ninja 2* brought all the acrobatic chop-socky action of those classic Sho Kosugi movies to home computers, and even added an air of quality that gave it a respectability beyond its creed.

Name	:	Cybernoid
Year	:	1988
Publisher	:	Hewson Consultants
Author	:	Raffaele Cecco, Nick Jones, J. Dave Rogers, John M. Phillips

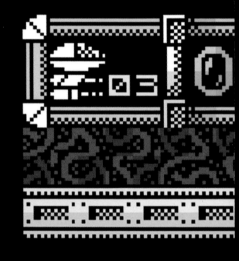

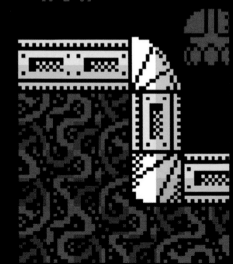

A in *Cybernoid*. We still feel as though we owe you an apology. A significant childhood lesson was learned here when we made the soul-crushing mistake of entering the cheat code on the very first game (typing 'WXY' into the menu screen, if heavy-hearted memory serves right). It sullied what would have been weeks, if no months of insanely superb scrolling shooter mirth. Where other games in this overfull genre kept the screen moving at a steady pace, forcing you to keep up or perish, *Cybernoid* played it screen-by-screen. This effectively lent the game something of a puzzle slant, as survival meant discovering safe passage through each unique room. Fortunately your ship was equipped with a delicious arsenal of awesome weaponry that, aside from some skilful flying and dexterous joystick waggling, provided the key to unlocking each new high-octane arena. Replenishing your stock of mines, missiles, bombs, shields and other delectable war tech was an important part of the gameplay, and helped make *Cybernoid* into the rich and beloved blaster it will always be remembered as.

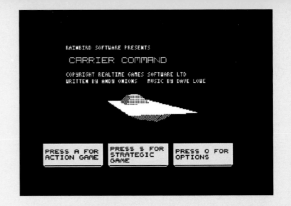

Name	:	Carrier Command
Year	:	1989
Publisher	:	Rainbird Software
Author	:	Andrew Onions, David Lowe, Derrick Austin

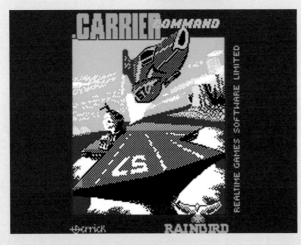

Although we now lament the days when the arcades went 3D and coin-op gaming ate itself, in 1988, sat in front of a Spectrum and a portable TV in our bedroom, the elusive third dimension was still a far-off dream. And then *Carrier Command* came along, and we were plunged into new depths of astonishing polygonal realism. *Carrier Command*, though somewhat forgotten by gaming scholars, was remarkable for a number of reasons. Yes, it featured hyper real (well, for the day) 3D vector graphics, but it also boasted a great sci-fi storyline. A team of scientists had created remote controlled aircraft carriers, and it was up to you to pilot them around an archipelago and colonise it. Naturally this involved destroying opposing aircraft carriers while usurping its occupied islands, which added some great action and to the strategic objective. By the way it's interesting to note that the lame-brain C64 couldn't handle filled vector graphics and had to resort to top-down visuals for its version of *Carrier Command*. Chalk up another point for the Speccy!

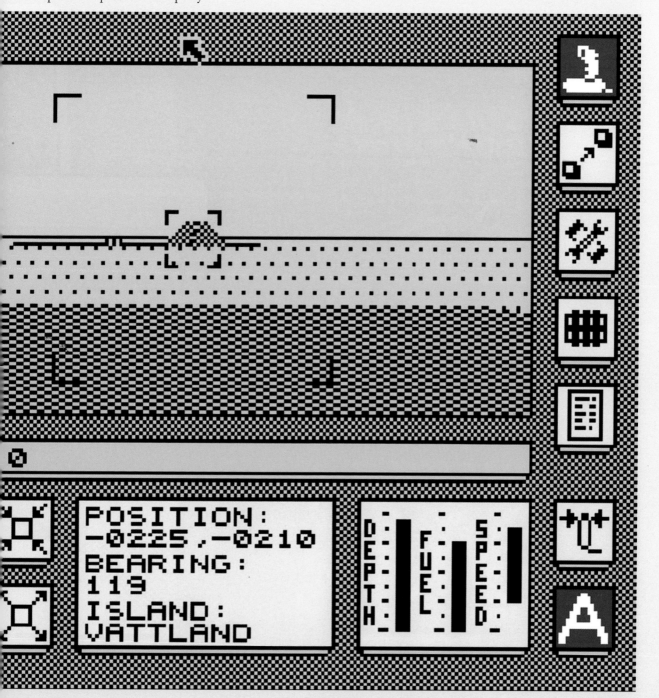

CHASE H.Q.

1. SINCLAIR JOYSTICK
2. CURSOR JOYSTICK
3. KEMPSTON JOYSTICK
4. KEYBOARD
5. DEFINE KEYS

Name	:	Chase H.Q.
Year	:	1989
Publisher	:	Ocean Software
Author	:	John O'Brien, Bill Harbison, Jonathan Dunn

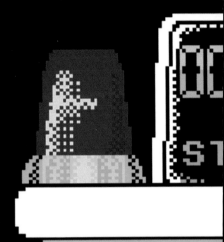

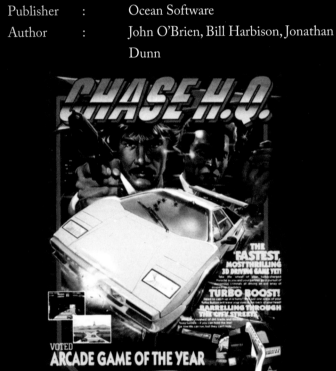

O*ut Run* had made driving games the coolest kids on the arcade floor and topping its Ferrari-powered awesomeness was proving extremely difficult. So Taito recruited a couple of Miami Vice lookalikes, stuffed them into a Porsche 928 and sent them out to rip up the highways in pursuit of vicious criminals making their daring getaways in equally cool cars. The brilliance of *Chase H.Q.* was its moving objective. You weren't racing toward a static finish line, but hunting down a fleeing criminal. Prang your car too often, or curb it on a badly-taken corner and not only do you lose points against the time, but your quarry increases the distance between you and them. Split second decisions had to be made as you tore toward the junctions, or risked shortcuts along dirt tracks, until you put expensive motor on the bumper of the perp and ran the sucker off the road. The driving mechanics and tracks of *Chase H.Q.* were quite superior to *Out Run*, too, making this the unequalled pinnacle of Spectrum driving games.

TAITO

© TAITO CORPORATION 1987
© GRAFTGOLD LTD 1989

CREDIT 1

Name	:	Rainbow Islands
Year	:	1990
Publisher	:	Ocean Software
Author	:	David O'Connor, John Cumming

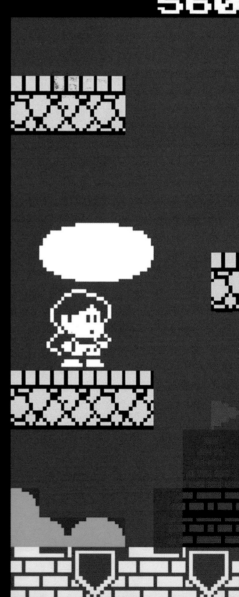

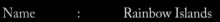

A more colourful loading screen, nay entire game, was never seen on the Spectrum than here, in the *Bubble Bobble* pseudo-sequel *Rainbow Islands*. Considered to be one of the best and most popular computer games ever (by the magazines and their readers of the day), the home conversions of this coin-op classic were universally superb. Though it's considered to be the follow-up to *Bubble Bobble*, you won't find any dragons, bubbles or two player modes here. Despite these apparent shortcomings, *Rainbow Islands* should be considered a monumental triumph in its own right. Climbing inexorably toward the top of the multi-platformed levels, a host of cute creatures, vehicles and monsters were dispatched by shooting them with a short-range rainbow or, in order to collect gems from their downfall, dropping a rainbow on them from above. These rainbows also served as easily collapsible bridges, aiding your ascent to the boss battle at the top. *Rainbow Islands* more than earned its status as one of the finest games ever made, and continues to live up to that glorious accolade.

Name   :   Midnight Resistance
Year   :   1990
Publisher :   Ocean Software
Author   :   Jim Bagley, Charles Davies, Keith
              Tinman

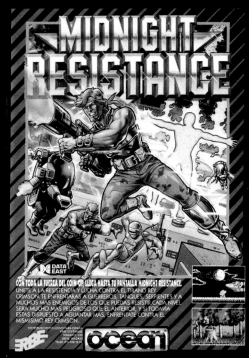

This was a tricky conversion for any home system, let alone the humble Spectrum. There was one major hardware limitation that might have stumped any developer other than the 8-bit maestros at Ocean and Special FX. You see, *Midnight Resistance* borrowed its coin-op joysticks from *Ikari Warriors*, which rotated in 360 degrees, alongside the usual directional mechanics. This allowed players to strafe in any direction, while moving in another. So it's even more impressive that the Spectrum's slightly redesigned *Midnight Resistance* was such a rip-roaring success when it came home. Two players turned the platformer, which moved in all directions, into a sensational war zone thanks to bucket fulls of nonstop action and great weaponry that included machine guns, shotguns, flamethrowers, missiles, scatterguns and more. Graphical limitations were deftly sidestepped by redesigning the characters into slightly more cartoony versions of their arcade selves, which also made enough room for plenty of Spectrum-style blocky colour.

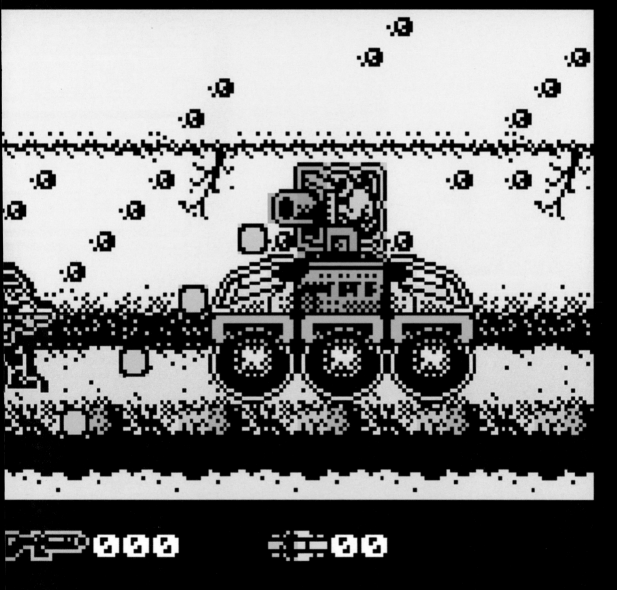

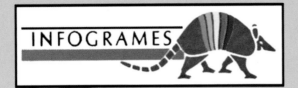

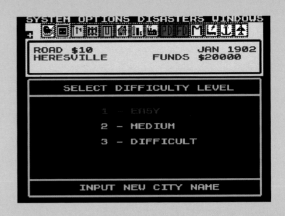

Name : Sim City
Year : 1990
Publisher : Infogrames
Author : Antony R. Lill, Simon Butler

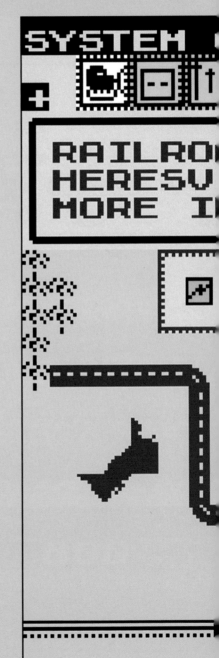

The Spectrum was under fire from 16-bit machines by 1990. People were looking toward massively detailed and in-depth games rather than more shooters and platformers. Games like *Sim City;* world builders that could never be condensed to fit on a cassette tape. Except the team at Probe Software accomplished this incredible task, and did it so well they made it appear that *Sim City* had been created with the Spectrum gamer in mind all along. *Sim City* was delivered intact, allowing you to become governor of your own sprawling 8-bit metropolis while proving that the brilliance of the game was in its design and not its flashy visuals. The modular design of the city management game was subtly adjusted to match the Speccy's blocky approach to graphics, and all the urban planning, power distribution and civil engineering was translated with elegance, as well as ergonomics. In many ways the very gameplay of *Sim City* mirrors the impressive feat of its Spectrum adaptation, and it was efforts like this that managed to keep the 8-bit computers alive for another few, wonderful years.

The front cover of
Issue 2 of Crash
magazine - KONG
by Oliver Frey.

THE MEMOIRS

Simon Butler

Simon spent many a year at the famous software house, Ocean Software, producing the graphics for some of their classic Spectrum titles - who can forget the detailed scenes within *The Never Ending Story* and the claustrophobic forest of *Platoon*.

I never owned a Spectrum; I never had any need.

Working in the industry meant that if I was in-house then I was plonked at a desk with a variety of machines ready for use, or one was provided to work off-site.

And while I would never go as far as to say that any one machine held sway over the others I will state for the record that the Spectrum holds a very special place in my heart.

Not for the games, although I certainly played my fair share, a lot of which shaped the way I see games, what they mean to me and what I expect from even the biggest of today's Triple-A products.

No, the Spectrum was the machine I truly enjoyed creating graphics on.

I certainly did my fair share of Commodore and Amstrad titles, all of which had their highs and lows, but the good old Spectrum (I shan't say humble) was about as close as you could get at that time to doing something akin to pencil and paper work.

It actually felt like you were drawing.

It certainly could be a temperamental little beast at times; shaky, often unreliable with added perils of saving to cassette, but it was small and unassuming unlike its big, brash American opponent.

It was quintessentially British and I suspect because of that it never reached the distant parts of the globe that it should.

But for all of that, or perhaps because of that it belongs to a generation of gamers, who I suspect are predominantly British and who, like me can't fail to smile every time they see one of these little rascals.

I think it's fair to say that the first game I worked on was *The Never Ending Story* and while I knew I couldn't hope to emulate the vivid and masterful images created

The Never Ending Story - released in 1985 by Ocean Software to coincide with the film of the same name.

by Steve Cain for the C64 version, I was determined to do my very best and I enjoyed every single moment.

I know exactly what room I was sitting in, I can see the table with graph paper and pencils; a habit I soon put aside for the sheer freedom and pleasure of just drawing on-screen.

And that is another thing that this funny black magical box means to me; freedom.

My career at that time was work-for-hire and I moved from one project to another, doing single or multiple versions of this game or that and even finding it possible to design original titles such as *Bounces*, *Cosmic Wartoad* and contribute to *Shadowfire*.

This freedom all but disappeared as the industry grew more corporate and the Licensed Product took a vice-like grip on creativity and strangled it near to death.

Happily today's indie scene has rekindled that can-do spirit so long missing from the soulless franchises we have been force-fed for the last two decades.

The pixel has returned and while it may never be as colourful as the Amstrad or as fuzzy and rectangular as those on the C64 the single black pixel of the Spectrum is a solid foundation under a strong and steadfast games catalogue that can stand alongside any other in the industry.

It drove me to despair at times with all-too regular crashes, it made me think while trying to work around the attribute problems, but it never failed to satisfy.

Hunchback - The Adventure, released in 1986 by Ocean Software.

Sprites I had no hand in creating still spring to mind in games such as *Target: Renegade*, *Sacred Armour* of *Antiriad*, *Knight Lore*, *Starquake*, *Nodes of Yesod*....the list goes on and on.

If asked to work on one of the 'old' machines again today, I would have no hesitation in choosing the Spectrum.

It is an old friend and like old friends I know it will be unreliable, tetchy and temperamental but will come through in the end and will always be well worth seeing again.

I never owned a Spectrum.

I'm glad.

If I had I think I would have found it impossible to say goodbye.

Dan Dare III - released in 1990 by Virgin Games and developed whilst at Probe Software.

Steve Wetherill

Steve's name is synonymous with the classic titles released by Odin Computer Graphics, namely *Nodes of Yesod*, *Robin of the Wood*, *Heartland* and *Sidewize*.

Over a 30-year career in video games, I have been fortunate to work for several successful companies on well-regarded games, but it all started for me with the ZX Spectrum.

As an Electrical Engineering student at Manchester 'Owens' University back in 1982, I remember reading many magazine advertisements for the Sinclair Spectrum, '16K or 48K RAM... full size moving-key keyboard... colour and sound... high-resolution graphics... From only £125'. At the time I was taking a Z80 assembler class at Manchester University and was using an RML380Z.

The next year, back home in Barnsley, I bought (with a lot of help from my Mum) a 16K Sinclair ZX Spectrum and a 13" black & white TV that totalled £200 in 1983 money from WH Smiths. My early recollections upon acquiring the Spectrum are spending hours and hours loading and exploring the *Horizons* tape, and then playing *Manic Miner*, *Lunar Jetman* and then later *Atic Atac*. I bought the computer primarily due to my interest in electronic music, but pretty soon I was trying to figure out how to make games in Z80. I remember disassembling *Time Gate* by Quicksilva, and the minor epiphany when I finally understood LDIR for block byte copies - thanks John Hollis!

Staying up into the wee small hours in the house on Airedale Road, Barnsley writing Speccy demos, I remember shivering in the unheated bedroom under the bedclothes with the black and white TV and the Spectrum and cassette tape player on my lap keeping me warm.

At this stage I was contemplating a career in

One of the first games that Steve played on his new ZX Spectrum was *Lunar Jetman* by Ultimate Play the Game.

video games, and had stepped up to using *OCP Full Screen Editor/Assembler*.

At the time, my main reading material was *Programming the Z80* (actually the Radio Shack edition called *How to Program the Z80*) by Rodney Zaks and *The Complete Spectrum ROM Disassembly* by Dr Ian Logan and Dr Frank O'Hara.

I soon figured out the XOR trick for drawing and erasing sprites. Then, using Z80's interrupt mode two for smooth sprite movement, I came up with a demo that I sent out to numerous companies. This led to an interview in 1983 with Software Projects in the Bear Brand Complex, Woolton, Liverpool and subsequently to my first job in games.

I stayed in a house in Holt Road, Higher Tranmere, Birkenhead and from there I'd catch the train at Green Lane station, under the Mersey to Liverpool, and from there catch the bus each day to Woolton Village. Stoo Fotheringham started at the same time as me carrying out pixel work for various Software Projects games.

I spent a year or so at Software Projects porting *Manic Miner* and *Jet Set Willy* to the Amstrad CPC with Derrick Rowson - my first published games. Derek and I never saw Matthew Smith's original Spectrum source code but we were decently equipped with Tandy TRS80 computers to pull off the job. We expanded the room count in the CPC version of *Jet Set Willy* to twice the Spectrum original (the Holt Road house featuring in some of the sewer related areas). Software Projects later ported the CPC version back to the Spectrum and released it as *Jet Set Willy 2*.

In late 1984 I left Software Projects for Paul McKenna's company, Odin Computer Graphics, based in Steers House, Canning Place, Liverpool. There, I joined Marc Wilding, Stoo Fotheringham, Colin Grunes and Paul Salmon and took the lead programmer role on

Nodes of Yesod was the first game Steve worked on after joining Odin Computer graphics, released in 1985.

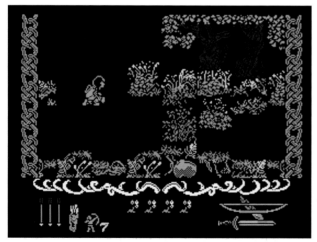

Robin of the Wood, released in 1985.

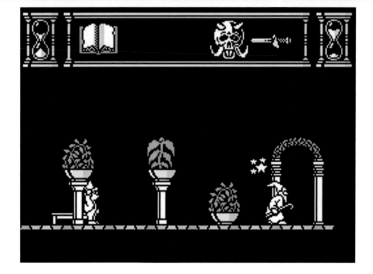

Heartland, released by Odin in 1986.

completing *Crosswize*, I joined Denton Designs, who were based on Rodney Street, Liverpool, next to the Midland Bank. Using a swanky ex-Imagine Sage IV machine to write the Z80 code, I worked on the Speccy version of *Foxx Fights Back* with Paul Salmon. *Foxx Fights Back* was the last Spectrum game I worked on.

That was not quite the end of my involvement with Spectrum games, however. Working with Paul McKenna, I published a 25th Anniversary Edition of *Nodes of Yesod* for the iPhone and Flash in 2010. I coded both the versions, which was a bit of a labor of love for me.

My career has brought me a long, long way from shivering under the bedclothes in Barnsley, but I still own my original rubber key Spectrum. Though super busy working at KIXEYE in San Francisco these days, I am eyeing the upcoming 30-year anniversary of *Nodes of Yesod in 2015*. On reflection however, it might be nice to give *Nodes* a break, and perhaps do a refresh of some of the other Speccy titles I worked on.

Nodes of Yesod, which was already looking beautiful with Colin's pixels. At Odin we used BBC model B computers with a w/Z80 second processor to write the Spectrum code.

Nodes shipped in 1985. After that I worked on *Robin of the Wood* with Paul Salmon - Paul providing pixels and design. Next came *Heartland* and *Sidewize*, with Colin Grunes pushing the pixels. *Heartland* was a very pretty looking game, which is all the more impressive when you consider that the artists at Odin used *Melbourne Draw* (drawing pixels one at a time, or at best using flood-fill) to create graphics for the Sinclair machine - a very skilled but laborious task.

After Odin's closure in 1987 I developed a *Sidewize* sequel, *Crosswize*, for Firebird with Colin, with Tony Beckwith producing at Firebird.

In early 1988, after

Sidewize, released by Firebird Software in 1987.

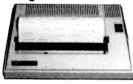

Roger Kean

Roger was the editor of the most iconic Spectrum related magazine of the 1980's and 1990's - *Crash*. Many a Spectrum fan looked forward to their dose of Sinclair news, reviews and the amazing covers by Oliver Frey.

Before Crash Micro Games Action was a twinkle in the eye, towards the end of 1982 Franco Frey introduced me to Clive Sinclair's astonishing box of tricks, the ZX Spectrum. It was a thing of beauty; such a simple design with an astonishing amount of power packed into its tiny (almost weightless) footprint. With hindsight, I can say that never was there a more elegant looking computer until Steve Jobs returned to Apple and began creating the new range of iMacs.

At the risk of bringing down the wrath of Gary Penn, Jaz Rignall and endless C64 adherents, in the Commodore 64 they played with a lump of beige-coloured fudge compared to the original Spectrum: shiny

3D Tank Duel, the original advertisement, created by Oliver Frey for Realtime.

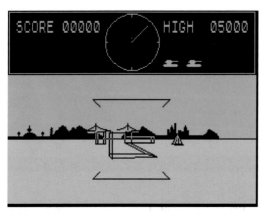

black carapace contrasted with the grained upper block, itself embossed subtly black-on-black with SINCLAIR, and below it in white, ZX Spectrum. And the lightning colour-band flash angled jauntily to cross from side to face in red, yellow, green and cyan. With these colours, Oliver Frey made Crash covers sing.

Some might have likened the Spectrum to a glorified calculator (though without a screen), but a closer inspection of the keyboard dispelled that – it more resembled the manuals of a giant church organ, scored with the mysterious runes of BASIC: in white on grey of PLOT, RUN, RAND, GOTO, POKE; underneath in red: VERIFY, FORMAT, SCREEN$; above in green: RESTORE, DATA, L PRINT, INKEY$. I had no idea what all that was about, but it looked exciting and gorgeous at the same time.

Fortunately, there were plenty about who did know what could be done with the arcane language of BASIC, and later with machine code. One who stands out (for the reason cited below) was Andy Onions. With

Realtime Software colleagues Ian Oliver and Graeme Bird he created a *Battle Zone*-style wireframe game that pushed the Spectrum to its limits and beyond. *3D Tank Duel* was the first of innumerable games which passed through the hands of Crash reviewers while in development and (hopefully) were improved as a result of the playtesting. Writing in June 1984 (the review appeared in the August issue of Crash, published in July, at press late June), the three reviewers gave it a combined overall rating of 83%, a pretty high score in those more parsimonious days – incidentally they were not the playtesters.

There was a personal aspect to Realtime (based in Leeds). Andy Onions's parents were neighbours in Old Street, Ludlow where Crash was put together (the move to King Street came soon after). Onions Senior owned The Old Firestation, a shop selling everything to do with fireplaces. On the floor above was a large renovated flat with several bedrooms, and this we rented on behalf of the increasing numbers of staff joining Newsfield from places as far apart as Cornwall, Aberystwyth, Manchester and London.

The *3D Tank Duel* experience was an aspect of working with the Spectrum that I enjoyed, communing with the programmers and publishers, because from top to bottom one thing was always apparent: the passion and sheer excitement at being at the start of something that felt like it could become enormous. I thought a great deal, and wrote about, the professional laziness of programmers at giant corporations like ICL (UK) and IBM (US), with acres of ROM and RAM at their fingertips, compared to the ingeniousness of the bedroom Speccy programmer. Working in an environment limited to 16K and 48K obliged them to invent and perfect the most amazing forms of compression –forerunners of the algorithms by which we today pack vast quantities of image data to fit into tiny storage spaces.

The Realtime boys were but a speck on the surface of the talent pool the Spectrum fostered, so many names it's hard to recall them all today, and probably unfair to pick any out for special mention, but in those early days two names impinged because these lads hung out with 'our lads' at the Personal Computer World shows: from Software Projects, *Manic Miner* and *Jet Set Willy* creator Matthew Smith; from Ocean *Hunchback's* Christian Urquhart. They embodied the spirit of the time.

In the years since, I've had many an interesting time, but few compare with the thrill that the Spectrum brought me in its sparkling wake. It is no exaggeration to say that the Spectrum propelled me into a life-change of magnitude.

Aliens over Ludlow: Newsfield and Crash founders Roger Kean, Franco Frey and Oliver Frey.

Paul Owens

Paul created some of Ocean Software's most iconic games. He started at the company from the very beginning and stayed for over 10 years. Early games included *Kong*, *Hunchback* and *Daley Thompson's Decathlon*.

I loved the Spectrum and I still do. I can still recall the first sensuous feel of those slightly stiff rubber keys of my first 16K. I wrote games for the Amstrad CPC and BBC, oh and the Tatung Einstein. I even dabbled on the VIC, Oric and Commodore 64, but none came close to the Spectrum. The Amstrad was a pale copy, the BBC was for mummy's boys and the Commodore, well they were for rich kids and too easy to write for with all their fancy sound chips and hardware sprites. No, the Spectrum was British and proud; it was a true geek's machine.

I grew up watching my father build racing cars called Chevrons and in 1973 a Formula 5000 Chevron beat all the Formula 1 cars in the race of champions. A car built by a few guys in a mill in Bolton thrashed all the big factory F1 teams. It was a proud moment in our family. The Sinclair machines appealed to me in a similar way as they are a British success built by a few guys in a shed in Cambridge. Albeit a big posh looking air-conditioned shed with expensive Z80 emulators and VAX mainframes – buy hey, you get my point.

My favourite Spectrum was the 128K +2 which had had a tiny amount of my input in its design. I helped Sinclair iron out some of the bugs or rather iron back in some of the good bugs into, what we call now, the operating system. When the Derby (the 128K Spectrum's working name) prototype was first cut, it wouldn't work with some early ZX Spectrum games and crashed in a random way. I was summoned to Sinclair to help and it turned out that, much to the surprise of the Sinclair boffins, the new prototype was missing some hardware foibles. When the first 16K Spectrum was designed, Sinclair had cut corners and things called CPU interrupt vectors were linked to any

Daley Thompson's Decathlon - Paul created the game with Chris Urquhart and it was published by Ocean Software in 1984.

old pin close by on the circuit board. Unknown at the time this shortcut would allow programmers to prevent flicker and make sounds. In the 128K, Sinclair had used the money earned from previous versions to engineer a better machine with no shortcuts and different boards. It was this that caused the problems. They re-engineered the early shortcuts back into the 128K and hey presto it worked. I'm still not sure why they released it in Spain first though.

My favourite game is a difficult one but I would say *Manic Miner*. It was not a direct arcade port and had some neat technical tricks to those in the know; particularly the in game music that was ground breaking at the time. It played well and was the first game I played all night, not counting one frustrating night with *The Hobbit* due to the consumption of our local's finest. I was working long hours writing one of the Daley Thompson games at the time and when your job is writing and then testing Spectrum games, playing other Spectrum games at night was not something we programmers normally did.

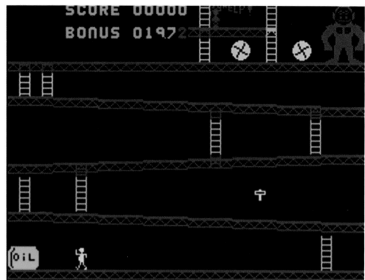

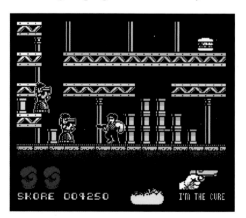

Manic Minor however had just the right amount of difficulty and reward to keep me hooked.

Jetpac was another that stands out, as the graphics just looked so much better than ours at Ocean Software but gameplay didn't last as long as I would have liked. *Chuckie Egg* also deserves a mention. My favourite games from our Ocean stables I would put as *Cobra*, written by Jonathan Smith. 'Joffa' was a mate and his quirky sense of humour shone through in the graphics.

The ZX Spectrum changed my life. I was all set to be a chemist or polymer technologist when along came the Sinclair ZX81 and then the Spectrum. I was trying to earn money during the summer break from University by writing games - I never went back. The Spectrum allowed me to make money doing something I enjoyed (programming) and I still do. Unfortunately it's not on the Spectrum any more.

One of Paul's early efforts for Ocean Software was *Kong*. Can you see the similarity to a well known arcade game?

Cobra on the Spectrum. Everyone wanted to know how Joffa achieved such smooth scrolling effects.

Mike Lamb

Mike teamed up with Dawn Drake to create some iconic games for Ocean Software including *Robocop*, *Target: Renegade* **and** *Batman: The Movie*. **Before his Ocean days, Mike programmed** *Steve Davis Snooker*.

I loved working on the Spectrum. There's a danger in looking back to your youth, that you put rose-tinted glasses on, but some things really were good and the Spectrum was one of them.

Most 8-bit machines like the NES and C64 had a character mapped display with hardware sprites.

If you were making games with sprites on a background (like most of the work I did at Ocean) then this architecture made for smoother, more colorful games. I never worked on the Commmodore 64 but it seemed as though there was a fairly obvious way to implement a game so long as you stayed within the hardware limitations. And if the game called for something beyond the limitations there wasn't much

Wec le Mans - released by Ocean Software in 1988.

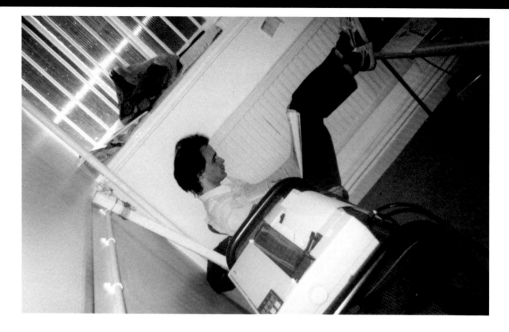

Mike taking a break from programming the next blockbuster.

you could do.

Maybe because the Spectrum was supposed to be an educational machine Sinclair went with a bit-mapped display. You had to print the background and sprites in software, but that made the Spectrum more flexible. There were a lot more opportunities to be clever. You could print the background using the stack and self-modifying code (like Jonathan

Smith) or cut animations into odd-shaped rectangles to save memory (like John Brandwood). Then there was stuff you couldn't do on character-mapped screens. My favourite Spectrum code was the track rendering routine for the *Wec le Mans* racing game.

The Z80 processor helped in that regard too. There were a lot more registers and instructions to play with than the 6502.

Looking back I think I overestimated the importance of this, but at the time it seemed better to work with 200 instructions instead of 20.

So that's what I liked about it. For the five years I worked on the Spectrum, there was always something new to try.

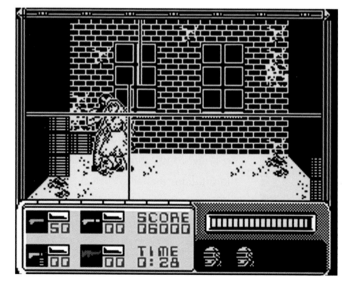

Robocop on the ZX Spectrum - graphics by Dawn Drake.

Jonathan Cauldwell

A veteran of the programming scene on the ZX Spectrum, Jonathan has released a huge number of games as well as utilities like *Arcade Game Designer* that allow enthusiasts to simply create their own game.

I don't remember the moment when I first decided to buy a computer, but it was probably sometime around September or October 1983. Back then, computers cost the proverbial arm and a leg, so if it had not been for Clive Sinclair I would probably never have owned one at all and my life would have turned out completely differently. Given my budget limitations, the choice was between the ZX81 and the increasingly popular ZX Spectrum.

I knew that the Spectrum was the better machine, but it would also take much longer to save the required money to purchase one. In the end, of course, the Spectrum won the day and it took until the following June before I had amassed £100. That was a fortune to a kid back then and

just enough to purchase a second-hand 48K machine with a dodgy power lead plus an added bonus of a couple of C60 cassette tapes stuffed full of games.

Those early days were special. Magical, even. It was as if Clive's little black box had opened a portal to an enchanted parallel universe. Going through the games on those C60s I really felt like the kid who had been given the keys to the sweet shop. The variety of games was impressive; I might be shooting enemy tanks in *Zzoom*, running a country in *Dictator* or rescuing islanders from an erupting volcano in *Escape from Krakatoa*. A few schoolfriends had recently obtained Spectrums too, and their games were equally exciting. We bought them, we swapped them, we copied them and talked about them endlessly. How might we escape from the Goblins' dungeon? How far could each of us get in *Pssst*? Had anyone visited The Yacht in *Jet Set Willy*? Break times, dinner times, class time, it didn't matter. When the final bell went at 3:45 I would dash home for a quick blast on *Astro Blaster* before another assault on *Invincible Island* or whatever other game was the playground vogue at the time.

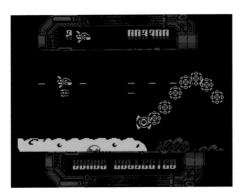

More Tea Vicar,
released in 2012.

It wasn't only about getting the latest must-have commercial game either, there were magazines packed with all manner of intriguing type-ins. Sinclair Programs listings were a good early way to learn about BASIC programming and I typed a few in, studied them and learned a few tricks. There were articles on programming as well; I borrowed magazines from others and before long started to pick up machine code, experimenting with my own games. It was a slow learning process but by the age of 16 I was starting to produce reasonable results and so began to sell some of them through lineage advertisements. That led on to writing games for Crash magazine cover tapes, then Sinclair User and Your Sinclair. Towards the end I was writing games for budget software houses, but by then the Spectrum games market had run out of steam and the remaining magazines folded, one by one.

Despite having received job offers to work on games for consoles I went straight into business software as a COBOL and occasional C programmer, although that was still only because the Spectrum had kindled an interest in software

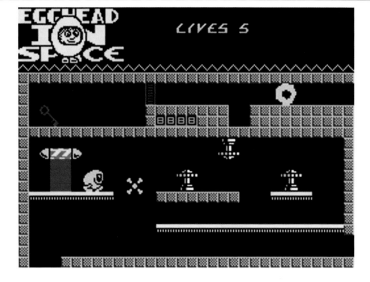

development generally. When I was made redundant some years later, JPM saw the Spectrum magazine cover tape games on my CV and employed me to write code for their fruit machines. That in turn led to my current job developing video games for Bell-Fruit, so you might say that things really have come full-circle. These days I get a little hardware assistance to move sprites around the screen, but the principles remain the same.

The Spectrum has shaped my life and helped to make me who I am, just as it shaped the games industry and set it on its initial course.

Developers who cut their teeth on the machine lived or died by the strength of their own code because they couldn't fall back on support chips. Its BASIC nature meant that it truly was a blank canvas that didn't force developers down a particular avenue; innovation flourished.

Three decades later it still is, and for a few of us still programming the machine today, it always will be.

Egghead in Space, one of many games Jonathan has written with Egghead as the main character, released in 2003.

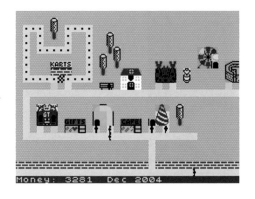

Fun Park, released in 2004 by Cronosoft.

Andrew Hewson

Andrew started his love affair with the Spectrum by writing books on the computer. The writing soon turned to publishing many classic games through the renowned Hewson Consultants Ltd.

I have a theory that all creativity comes from technological development. Whether it's the invention of the printing press, the arrival of electronic guitars and synthesisers in the 1960s, or the introduction of the first iPhone in 2007, the pattern is always the same. First you get the technology and then an explosion of creativity inevitably follows.

The ZX Spectrum was not the first games machine in the UK, but it was a major turning point for the UK home computer market and was instrumental in bringing gaming into the mainstream.

Before it arrived we were an embryonic industry serving a growing niche of enthusiasts. Machines like the ZX80 and the ZX81 had taken us to that point, but their wider success was still tempered by their clunky design and rudimentary performance. When the ZX Spectrum came along we reached a tipping point.

The keys on the ZX80 and the ZX81 were just horrible, so when the ZX Spectrum arrived the spongy keys were the first thing you noticed after the rainbow stripe at the bottom right of the machine.

The first time I saw a Spectrum was at one of the ZX Micro Fairs in London. I remember pushing those spongy keys, which still weren't great, and thinking 'well, they're better than the ZX81!'. But it soon turned out that they were good enough.

Once you got past the keys it was clear that the Spectrum was

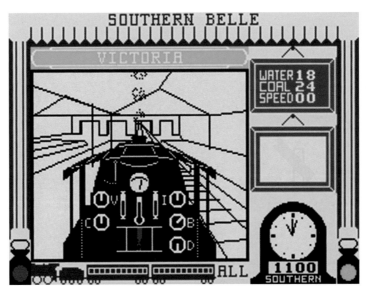

Southern Belle, a train simulator published by Hewson Consultants in 1985.

an evolution of the ZX81 across the whole system. Same Z80 chip, same built-in BASIC soft-wired into the keyboard, same memory layout. But now we had 16K, or even 48K, of RAM, colour instead of monochrome graphics and all while maintaining that crucial low price point. It all came together beautifully to create a machine that was more than the sum of its parts and lifted everything to a level where suddenly it was catching the attention not just of the enthusiasts but also of the man on the street.

In the UK market, Sinclair had the first mover advantage. Other home grown machines appeared – the Dragon, the Jupiter Ace and others I can barely remember – but Sinclair already had a user-base and, crucially, the support of activists like me who were trying to build businesses on the back of his machines. Sinclair's true rivals in the market came from the US in the form of the Commodore C64 and the Atari console but I think it is fair to say that without Clive Sinclair's determination to create a 'good enough' machine at a bargain price, there would have been no UK games industry.

The result was that the market suddenly opened up. Retailers like WH Smith really got behind the machine. They stocked the Spectrum and the

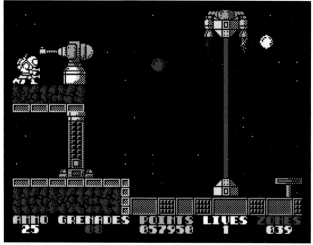

Exolon, written by Raffaele Cecco and published by Hewson Consultants in 1987.

games, they even stocked programming guide books like mine. Suddenly the whole thing had momentum. The market was expanding, the games were selling in greater numbers than ever before and most importantly they were becoming more and more sophisticated. We were very fortunate to be working with some incredibly talented programmers and they began to take things to a whole new level.

Steve Turner started off by writing some cracking arcade games for us and

Zynaps, another great side scrolling game from Hewson, published in 1987.

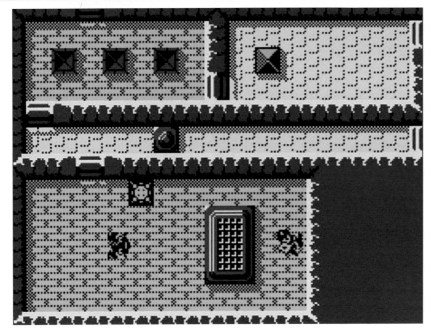

Ranarama, one of the many titles programmed by Steve Turner for Hewson Consultants, published in 1989.

power elsewhere. I don't need a walking animation for the enjoyment of the game.'. However, before the ZX Spectrum a game like *Avalon* would simply not have been possible. It was the machine itself which unleashed Steve's talent.

The ZX Spectrum wasn't the first games machine in the UK, but it was a technological leap which undoubtedly led to a surge in creativity. For us that began with games like *Avalon* and continued right into the early nineties with the likes of *Ranarama*, *Dragontorc*, *Quazatron*, *Technician Ted*, *Exolon*, *Cybernoid*, *Zynaps* and *Stormlord*. Our role was to allow the geniuses who created these games to do what they do best and support them in whatever way we could, but it was the ZX Spectrum itself which opened the door, because all creativity comes from technological development.

then I remember him telling me 'I'm working on a Dungeons and Dragons style of game'. So I said 'okay, great... whatever you want to do!'.

When I saw *Avalon* for the first time it was a sensation! He had this wonderful colour border effect creating a kind of theatre stage with the dungeon set inside and a wizard floating around on a carpet. Steve explained to me that he'd done it that way so as to avoid the need to animate the wizard walking around the dungeons because there isn't enough processing power in the system.

To my mind that was the genius of coders like Steve, the ability to say 'No, I don't want that problem. I'm going to push it aside and have the wizard floating on a carpet so I can use that processing

The loading screen to *Stormlord*, published in 1989.

Transform your Spectrum now!

Transform your Spectrum now with the FDS Keyboard, the best selling Spectrum keyboard in the U.K. The Fuller FDS Keyboard with its stylish, slim-line appearance gives you the look and feel of a real microcomputer keyboard and helps you enter data with lightening fast accuracy.

The keyboard contains all the graphic characters of your ZX Spectrum plus additional function keys. It has 4 cursor control keys, an auto rub-out key, a separate key for full stop and comma, a full length space bar, shift keys either side and 2 function keys for direct entry into green and red E modes.

The microdrive is easily adapted to go inside along with the power supply. Fixing is simplicity itself, no soldering or technical knowledge is required. For the user who is reluctant to install his Spectrum circuit board inside the FDS, a buffer is available (£8.75 + 80p p&p) which simply plugs into the expansion port and connects directly to the FDS Keyboard, allowing the whole cased Spectrum to be installed inside.

£49.95
+ £2.50 p&p

MICRO SYSTEMS

Fuller Micro Systems
The ZX Centre, 71 Dale Street,
Liverpool 2. Tel: 051-236 6109.

At Fuller Micro Systems we strive to maintain the highest quality in both research and development, ensuring our products are the very best. We have now built a brand new mail order department to ensure our service is also the very best. Our stock includes a full range of components and kits that will make the most of your Spectrum, all our products enjoy an excellent reputation for reliability and carry a world wide one year guarantee.

Jon Ritman

Jon has programmed many classic titles on the ZX Spectrum - his best titles are those where he paired up with Bernie Drummond on graphics - *Batman*, *Match Day 2* and *Head Over Heels*.

I will always know the Spectrum as the Speccy, that is how I will always remember it.

For me the Speccy was a true revelation even though it was my second computer, the ZX81 being the first. When I first got hold of my own Spectrum I was overwhelmed by how much new stuff there was to learn - the complex display layout; the almost useless interrupt system – the list goes on.

For all these problems it was a great little machine for the freedom it gave to the developer. So many other machines directed you to make a certain sort of game - they had hardware sprites and scrolling screens and everybody made games that, surprisingly, had hardware sprites and scrolling screens. Not on the dear old

3D Combat Zone, published by Artic Computing in 1983.

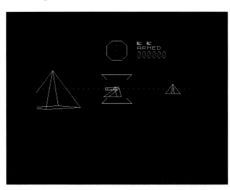

Speccy. We had no extra luxuries - we had open hardware and we programmed whatever we could imagine - and imagine was exactly what we did.

Initially most of us developers just produced copies of arcade games (and the programming community learned a great deal in the process), but it wasn't long before innovation began to grow. Sandy White's *Ant Attack* should be singled out here, a programming milestone even though it didn't attract the attention it deserved.

For myself I suspect I made the Spectrum's first full 3D game albeit a copy of the arcade classic *Battlezone* (*3D Combat Zone*) – I remember well seeing my first 3D rotating cube on screen, an absolute magic memory that may not seem much nowadays but remember there were no books or the internet back then with knowledge of how to do this.

A few games later I created the first 'good' football game (*Match Day*) for the Spectrum. I starting writing the game without a clue how to create the AI for such a game so left it until last. I wrote a ten line piece of code that simply held the following instructions: If you don't have the ball run towards it; if you do have the ball kick it up the field. That was it - not even a kick the ball towards the goal. I ran the code and the AI scored a goal against me in under 30 seconds. I actually cried with relief, laughing simultaneously. This was life as a games programmer in Speccy times as invention was a daily process as we were faced with challenges that were frequently the first time that anybody had ever had to solve – all in the drive to bring a cool game to market.

Match Day published by Ocean Software in 1984.

It was a fantastically innovative time. I well remember delivering the master copy of *Match Day* to Ocean Software, and handing it over to David Ward, one of the two directors. He in return handed me a game that Ocean were distributing for Ultimate Play the Game and told me that I had to take a look at it. I was going to see another games company that evening, Crystal Computing (later Design Design)

that I knew well and whilst there we loaded up the game and several jaws hit the floor - the game was the fabulous *Knight Lore*. I looked at it and knew I wanted to use the same technique in a game as to me it was a Disney cartoon come to life in a game. Needless to say I didn't have a clue how to go about doing such a 3D game. Over the next few months I racked my brains and spent endless late evenings

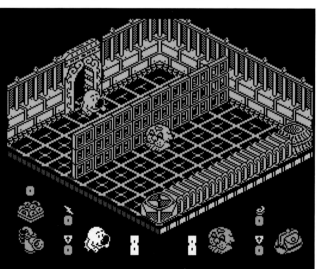

working out how to create an engine similar to *Knight Lore* – the engine I created was ultimately used in *Batman*. That's how it was for those early game programmers, someone would come up with a method, a new innovation; others would see it and improve it. It was a fantastic time; I'm so glad I was there.

Head Over Heels, published by Ocean Software in 1987.

Philip & Andrew Oliver

Philip and Andrew Oliver, best known as 'The Oliver Twins', started writing games back in their bedroom in the 1980s and have been in the industry ever since.

Fantasy World Dizzy, published by Code Masters in 1989.

Andrew and I had first been inspired to make games by Sinclair's ZX81. We'd wanted a colour computer after this and moved on to a Dragon 32, then a BBC Micro and finally an Amstrad CPC 464 before we returned to the Sinclair camp. Our first Spectrum, a 48K version, was a gift from Richard & David Darling the owners of Code Masters in October '86 - we were very late to this computer.

We'd just written *Super Robin Hood* in around a month for Codemasters on the Amstrad and it was selling very well. We were working on another game,

Ghost Hunters, and they thought it would be great if we could produce it on the Spectrum as well.

By now the Spectrum was the most popular home computer in the UK. It was running on the Z80 chip, the same as the Amstrad, so we figured it should be fairly similar to code for and that our games could be converted fairly quickly as a result. The Spectrum didn't have a Disk Drive, but our Amstrad did, so we asked a friend who knew some electronics to produce a method of sending code from the Amstrad to the Spectrum via the printer port. This was a breakthrough! We were able to write games for the Spectrum much more easily than almost everyone. We bought a second Amstrad, a CPC6128 with its really cool keyboard, hard drive and memory, and even used a ROM compiler (Maxam). So we could very quickly and easily write code, save it, and send to the Spectrum

and if it crashed we'd fix the bugs and have it running again within minutes. For the next three years we knuckled down and wrote many more Spectrum games (along with Amstrad versions) which all did extremely well.

Both *Super Robin Hood* & *Grand Prix Simulator* had already started development with other people prior to our Spectrum turning up, so we didn't write the Spectrum versions of these. We still have that first 48K Spectrum and it reminds us of great times - even if we didn't get much sleep!

It was a time when our friends had all gone to university and we'd talked our parents into allowing us to take a year out before going as well, which was expected of us, and to try and make a business and career out of making games. We were on a mission to prove we could do it.

What was great about writing games at that time was being able to write what you wanted without others telling you

Phil and Andrew Oliver - The Oliver Twins - at work in 1988.

what you could and couldn't do. We'd have an idea for a game inspired by a clever programming technique, maybe some ideas in another game, or something from real life and we thought, 'we could make a game of that'. We've always been impulsive and impatient and we wanted to quickly finish what we were working on so we could move onto this new idea we'd thought of. We saw other programmers around us at that time who would either get excited by the next idea and abandon their current work, for this 'new' idea. Some were forever trying to perfect their game, but actually, never releasing it, knowing with more effort they could make it better. We always set our sights on something that could be realistically programmed in around six weeks and we'd

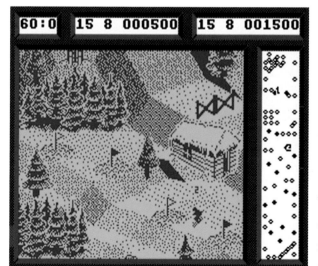

Professional Ski Simulator, published by Code Masters in 1987.

make damn sure we finished it before we moved on.

The thing that dogged every creator of Spectrum games was the 'attribute clash'. One thing that was 'fun' (a real challenge!) was creating the loading screens. We'd generally make the loading screen a copy of the box art that was created whilst we were writing the game. Which looking back now seems odd to us. But we'd show the Darlings a demo of the game we were working on and the next week they would be showing us a picture or two of how the box art could look and then we'd incorporate that back into the game via the loading screen. But trying to copy full colour artwork back into a Spectrum screen was always a challenge - check out *BMX Simulator 2* remembering the full colour illustration came first.

We loved the fact that these computers were technically limited. It was a game in itself trying to fit the idea you had into such a limited amount of memory. Around 32K, once the screen memory was taken away. For example, we had such big maps for Dizzy and trying to come up with ways to store the data with the absolute minimum amount of bytes was a fun challenge. Technical constraints like speed, memory and colour clash each made for interesting puzzle solving in its own right.

The best thing about making those games was knowing that WE, just the two of us, made them from start to finish - we came up with the ideas, wrote the games, did the art and within a matter of weeks they'd be in the shops. And if they weren't already on the 'best sellers' shelf, we'd move them there ourselves. There was no real interference, politics, unnecessary delays, paperwork or approvals.

We miss the simplicity of writing those games, but we wouldn't change that for the games and experiences we're able to create now with the amazingly talented team at Radiant Worlds in Warwick and today's technology.

Philip and Andrew's original design drawing for *Fantasy World Dizzy*.

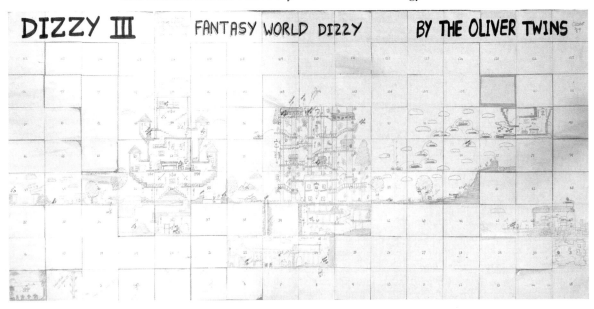

sinclair
ZX Spectrum

SOFTWARE AND PERIPHERALS CATALOGUE

June 1983 edition

Mevlut Dinc

Programming *Gerry the Germ* was a risky endeavour for Mev, it was not to everyone's taste. It's *Last Ninja 2* that Mev will be remembered for - a faultless conversion of a title that many thought could not be done.

The ZX Spectrum is what started it all for me in gaming, so it holds a special place in my heart!

My involvement with writing games was a complete accident as was my coming and living in England.

From 1980 I started working in Standard and Telephones Company, a cable factory in Southampton. I had no interest in games at all and absolutely no knowledge of computers.

I was very unhappy working at a factory and moaning about it all the time! A close workmate Vino Dos Santos eventually convinced me to get this new amazing computer called the ZX Spectrum, presumably hoping it would occupy my mind and shut me up!

Vino actually drove us to the Sinclair factory to pick up our beloved Spectrums, which were 16K.

A few weeks

Gerry the Germ,
Mev's first game published by Firebird Software in 1985.

later, we went back to the factory again, and I somehow managed to convince the receptionist to allow us to swap our Spectrums with the 48K ones from the pile at the reception!

Since I really had no real interest in gaming or computing accordingly I did nothing with my Speccy for weeks. But Vino kept asking me if I liked it, did I play this game and that, and in the end I thought just as well I should set it up and start playing around with it.

So, this is how it all started for me.

It was very tough at first as there was very little resource. I could not really make much of the information in the manual that came with the machine. It was 1983 and there was no internet – no nothing!

So, to cut a long story short, I learnt how to program the Spectrum in machine code in about 2 years, all from books and magazines. Popular Computing Weekly was my biggest source of inspiration and information.

My first game was *Gerry the Germ*, and as it was my first attempt, I wanted it to be unique, so I decided to base it around an anti-hero whose mission was to destroy a human body.

I showed a demo of *Gerry the Germ* to a number of publishers, but only Tony Rainbird at Telecomsoft showed genuine interest despite the controversial subject matter. For example, when I took it to to Mirrorsoft, they turned it down immediately saying they considered the premise to be in very bad taste.

I found games programming absolutely fascinating and very exciting, creating a product out of nothing was just a miracle

for me. In a really strange way I had absolutely no interest in playing games other than just checking them out to see what they were like, and how well they were designed and coded!

To this day I have hardly played any games at all, and admittedly I am absolutely useless at it, which is probably the main reason!

I could have easily started with a Commodore 64 but I am glad I ended up with the Spectrum. Although both machines have strengths and weaknesses I really enjoyed coding on the Speccy. There was no hardware support, no sound chip or anything so you had to code and create everything. It was all very challenging and fascinating to discover new ways and clever

Mev programmed the conversion of *Last Ninja 2* onto the Spectrum, published by System 3 Software in 1988.

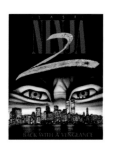

Big Trouble in Little China, published by Electric Dreams Software in 1987.

Knightmare, published by Activision in 1987.

techniques to keep pushing the machine to its absolute limit.

I was influenced by a couple of games technically and always tried very hard to do things better.

The Spectrum screen was really in a weird format and difficult to plot graphics on efficiently. So, I was over the moon when I discovered that I could use a pre-calculated screen address table and point the stack pointer to it.

Using techniques like this and many others I discovered I could make the Spectrum sing, literally. I wrote a music editor/sound driver, and my good friend musician Brian Marshall did some of the best Spectrum music ever using it.

I also developed the first ever scrolling isometric 3D game on the Spectrum, *Prodigy*.

One of my biggest early achievements was to do the Amstrad version of the amazing *Enduro Racer*. For some reason

the original developers did not want to do it and my good mates Rod Cousens and Jon Dean asked (begged more like!) me to do it. Using all my expertise and knowledge of the Spectrum I managed to get the original Spectrum code working on the Amstrad in about 3 weeks, and more importantly completed the entire development in a short while, in time for Christmas.

Of course, I am also very proud to be the programmer of *Last Ninja 2* on the ZX Spectrum, one of the most important games ever in my opinion. It was a massive challenge for me especially since the original C64 version was such a huge hit in every aspect and the original *Last Ninja* failed to come out on the ZX.

I was involved with the development and design of *Last Ninja 2* from day one and it was my job to make sure that the Spectrum version was every bit as good as the C64. I would like to think that I succeeded in achieving this goal. This also resulted in meeting with some great people in the industry namely Mark Cale, John Twiddy and Hugh Riley. I subsequently went on to set up Vivid Image Developments with John and Hugh.

Of all the systems I have worked on over a 30 + year career, the Sinclair ZX Spectrum holds the fondest memories for me; after all, I learnt everything about programming and designing games on the little machine. Thank you Vino and Sir Clive.

sinclair special   3

Inside...
The New ZX Microdrive!
Latest software...
Latest prices...

Steve Turner

Whilst at Hewson Consultants, Steve created many
classic titles for the Spectrum, including popular classics
3D Space-Wars, *Avalon* and it's follow-up, *Dragontorc*.

3D Seiddab Attack,
published by Hewson
Consultants in 1984.

I was a commercial COBOL and
IBM assembler programmer when
the Spectrum was announced. I had
already bought a ZX80 and tried to write
games for it but was defeated by the way
the CPU was used to display the screen;
when you ran code the display turned off.
I was just finding a way around this after
disassembling the operating system by
hand and reverse engineering the machine.
I had an asteroid flying across the screen
but had to make sure every path through
my code was exactly the right number of
machine cycles to synchronise with the
display to prevent the picture rolling like
a primitive TV set that needed adjusting.
The arrival of the ZX81 made my attempts
obsolete and I was so fed up I gave up -
until I saw a review of the forthcoming
Spectrum. With its high screen resolution
and colour I knew it was a games writer's
dream and this time I was determined to be
one of the first to write for it.

I can remember opening the box for
the first time and seeing the neat black
case and the little rubber keys, a vast
improvement on the ZX80. It came with
a thick manual which I eagerly searched
for information on how to use machine
code. My first task was to program a way
of developing a machine code program. I
didn't want to write an assembler, it would
take too long and soon they would become
available, so I wrote my first program
called *HexAutoloader*. It allowed you to
write code in BASIC REM statements. It
grabbed the code characters and converted
them into hexadecimal and put them in
RAM. I put in a system of labels so I could
jump to, or call code at a label, or refer to
variables rather than have to work out the
address every time the code changed. So
my input code had lines like REM 3E @
HITS. This first program was in assembler
poked into memory. I then let it load and
run itself which then allowed me to modify
it more easily. My first programs were
written using this program. It meant I had
to convert source code to the hexadecimal
loaded code by hand. I did this with the
aid of a couple of look up tables that listed
all the instructions in a couple of grids. I
used to write my source code on squared
paper in pencil, rubbing it out when it
changed. The hand assembled object code
was written in a column to the right of the

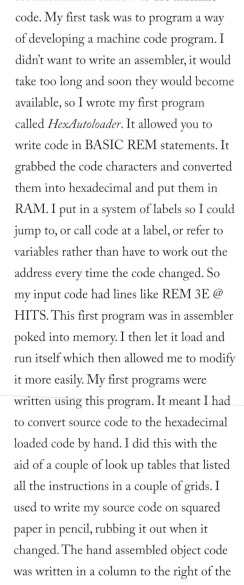

page. Debugging was a matter of checking your code over and over and dry running it. Later Andrew wrote a little monitor routine that I copied. It allowed you to dial up an address and look at the memory there while the code was running, or stop and start the code. This allowed us to tune up games while they were running by tweaking different variables.

I remember typing in the code on the rubber keyboard. My first Spectrum was only 16K so I soon had to fit a RAM expansion. If you hit the key too hard the RAM pack would wobble and the Spectrum would reset losing all the typing - so I became more tense with every line I typed. Frequent saves onto a cassette tape were necessary. I used an old wire coat hanger to fashion a clip to hold the RAM pack in place. It was a time of makeshift solution, but later I changed to a 48K machine. I programmed *3D Space Wars* in the evenings and in about six weeks had a playable game. I sent it to three publishers and two offered contracts. When I realised how much I could make from a game I handed in my notice and started full time

game programming. Unlike other games programmers I worked strictly nine to five with an hour lunch. It soon became a bit lonely working on my own so I asked Andrew Braybrook to join me. He used to program on the Dragon 64 which with its proper keyboard seemed a real computer compared to the Spectrum. The Speccy held its own with its bright colours and its versatility.

The Spectrum is a lovely machine to write for. There is little to learn in the way the machine works. You achieve things by mastering the Z80 assembler language. It soon became clear that speed was of paramount importance if you wanted to move a lot of graphics about. Every program I wrote improved on the speed of my first graphics routines. Programmers swapped ideas and we ended up using the Z80 in ways the chip designers never intended, such as clearing memory using the stack to make use of its fast auto increment of the address. I liked the way you

Avalon, published by Hewson Consultants in 1984.

3D Space-Wars, published by Hewson Consultants in 1983.

could change something on the screen with a single instruction. I can remember the restrictions of 48K. It meant you had to stop coding when you had filled the machine up. I used to spend days searching for code I could reduce in size so I could add a new routine or apply a fix.

The downside of the Spectrum was its character colour resolution and the limited sound. Clever design minimised the limitation of the colour. I used to make sure static parts of the screen were very colourful and contrasted to the moving area which had to be limited to prevent clashing of colours. The sound beeper could be made to play interesting sounds but only at a cost of execution time. Most games used a system of playing a little segment of sound then running the game for a cycle. I found a way of playing more than one note at once with two simultaneous timing loops. I used to make the two notes nearly the same to get a thick phasing effect which became my signature Spectrum music sound.

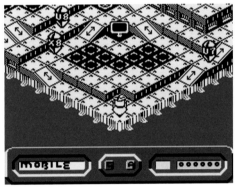

Quazatron, published by Hewson Consultants in 1986.

When ZX Microdrives were available I ordered a couple but could not get them to work reliably. I used to save five generations of changes on different tapes and still managed to lose work. I remember posing for a picture with a hammer about to smash the Microdrives. I didn't actually smash them; I sent them back for a refund. I eventually found a 5-inch disk drive that worked really well.

I also mounted the Spectrum board in a real keyboard. This made typing a lot easier although the connectors for the disk and joystick had to be piggy backed so after a while they could work loose and the machine crashed but at least the disk was much quicker to reload.

Later I was using a PC to assemble on and downloaded code to the Spectrum using a printer interface craftily rewired so I could set it to input or output. Somehow each improvement in technology diminished the magic of that little black box whose shell lay discarded in a drawer. Later, when all the writing had worn off the added keyboard, I rebuilt the original 48K Spectrum and still have it. It lead me into 15 years of developing games. It amazes me that the games are still around; 35 years later I still get fan mail.

My favourite Spectrum developments looking back were *Avalon* and *Dragontorc*. I can remember the feeling of pushing the edge, knowing I was doing something I had never seen. I drew mock rooms on paper and cut a rectangular hole from another sheet so I could see what the look would be like by moving the picture behind the frame. It reminded me a bit of a theatre set. I modelled the wizard character in plastacine and then drew him from eight angles. Andrew and I tested the games by playing them through from start to finish - with no cheats. That is the only way to really test playability.

New - the official Spectrum Upgrade!
Turn your Spectrum into a Spectrum + for just £20

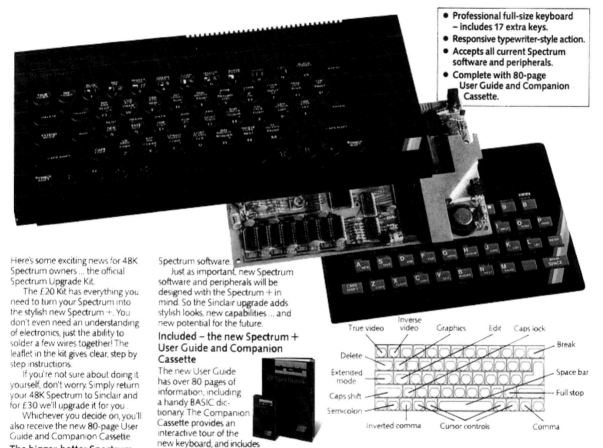

- Professional full-size keyboard – includes 17 extra keys.
- Responsive typewriter-style action.
- Accepts all current Spectrum software and peripherals.
- Complete with 80-page User Guide and Companion Cassette.

Here's some exciting news for 48K Spectrum owners ... the official Spectrum Upgrade Kit.

The £20 Kit has everything you need to turn your Spectrum into the stylish new Spectrum +. You don't even need an understanding of electronics, just the ability to solder a few wires together! The leaflet in the kit gives clear, step by step instructions.

If you're not sure about doing it yourself, don't worry. Simply return your 48K Spectrum to Sinclair and for £30 we'll upgrade it for you.

Whichever you decide on, you'll also receive the new 80-page User Guide and Companion Cassette.

The bigger, better Spectrum keyboard

The Spectrum + measures 12½" x 6". It has a large typewriter-style keyboard, with hard, moulded keys.

You'll find the new keyboard has a smooth, positive action – ideal for touch-typing, word processing, simulation programs, and extended programming sessions. Two retractable legs give a perfect typing position.

There are 58 keys in all, including 17 new keys. Programmers will be pleased to see dedicated punctuation keys, a space bar, and separate shift keys for graphics and extended modes. And a reset button allows you to clear a program from your computer's memory without disconnecting the power supply.

The official Spectrum Upgrade

Naturally your upgraded computer will accept all the peripherals in your Sinclair system - Interface 1, Microdrives and so on - as well as all

Spectrum software.

Just as important, new Spectrum software and peripherals will be designed with the Spectrum + in mind. So the Sinclair upgrade adds stylish looks, new capabilities ... and new potential for the future.

Included – the new Spectrum + User Guide and Companion Cassette

The new User Guide has over 80 pages of information, including a handy BASIC dictionary. The Companion Cassette provides an interactive tour of the new keyboard, and includes three entertaining arcade games.

TO ORDER BY MAIL:

When ordering the Upgrade Service, send off your 48K Spectrum to the address below, carefully wrapped, together with the completed coupon and appropriate payment. (Please do not return the mains adaptor, manual or other ancillaries.) Your upgraded computer will be despatched to you within 10 days of receiving your order.

When ordering the Upgrade Kit, simply complete the coupon, enclosing the appropriate payment and post it to us at the address below. Please allow up to 28 days for delivery.

BY PHONE: Access or Barclaycard holders can call Camberley (0276) 685311 for personal attention, 9am to 5pm Monday to Friday. Only the Upgrade Kits can be ordered by phone.

Please note: the upgrade offer applies to working 48K Spectrum models in the UK only.

True video · Inverse video · Graphics · Edit · Caps lock · Break · Delete · Extended mode · Space bar · Caps shift · Full stop · Semicolon · Inverted comma · Cursor controls · Comma

Sinclair Research Limited,
Upgrade Department,
Stanhope Road, Camberley,
Surrey. GU15 3PS.

Simon Hardy-Francis

Simon only wrote one game for the ZX Spectrum, the popular title *Critical Mass* for Durell Software back in 1985.

I wrote *Critical Mass* when I was 17 while working in my first fully employed job at Durell Software in Taunton, Somerset; one of the few computer game publishers in the South West of England. This was an exciting time because I had quit college and A Levels, moved out of home, and was living and working with other young developers of a similar age.

Looking back I was so green but I didn't feel green at all! After all, I'd already been programming since teaching myself and selling my first game at age 11. My brothers and I did a deal with the parents to buy a Dragon 32 which involved each of us committing the budget for two birthdays and a Christmas present towards the new computer. While my brothers played games all the time, I concentrated

Critical Mass, the tape cover above and to the right a photoshoot for Crash magazine to promote the game.

on programming with the games written in BASIC with assembler routines to help out. I couldn't afford the 6809 assembler cartridge – which was nearly as expensive as the Dragon itself - so just wrote the opcodes out on paper and calculated the relative jumps myself. The opcodes went into BASIC 'DATA' statements and were 'POKE'd into memory, and then 'EXEC'd.

I also went to school with the – now famous – Richard and David Darling of Codemasters fame, and spent several summers with my best friend Richard hanging out and hacking on his Commodore VIC 20 (which he brought over from Canada) and later the Commodore 64. We were also in the same classes at school and so spent a lot of time together.

Later I switched from the Dragon 32 to the Amstrad CPC which is how I got in contact with Durell - they themselves having a contract with Amsoft to create some games for the new home computer.

So six or seven years later – and after much programming on the Dragon 32, VIC 20, C64, and

Amstrad CPC – enter 'The Speccy' and my first full time job. By this time the Speccy was very established. It was relatively cheap compared to the other home computers and had sold in larger numbers. A best selling Speccy title could make the author rich, and I witnessed this first hand with Clive Townsend and his hit game *Saboteur*, so it was a very exciting time indeed.

On a technical level the Speccy also marked a new and important technical milestone in my career. Up until then I'd been developing games using the device itself and its built in storage, whether cassette tape or floppy disk. However, fast 286 PCs with Z80 assembler cross compilers were available at affordable prices which meant that it was possible to develop for the Speccy as if it were an embedded device; edit and compile the code on the very fast PC and then download and test it on the Speccy itself via a custom cable. I remember blowing up a Speccy or two myself while experimenting with the custom cable.

This was also my first time using a 'big boy' editor on a PC. Today there's possibly hundreds of editors for programmers but back then the choices were very limited. It

sounds incredible to any developer today, but I learnt how to program in the vacuum of the South West only knowing a few other developers and not having access to all the books, internet resource and open source that we have today.

Critical Mass was my first game that used any kind of indentation in the source code - and code comments, for that matter. It's amazes me today to think that I programmed for so many years without a single tab or comment.

With *Critical Mass* I tried very hard to push the technical boundaries of the Spectrum graphically. I believe it was the first game title to show off full screen scrolling on the Speccy. This was difficult to achieve because, unlike other home computers such as the C64, the Speccy had no hardware support for rendering graphics. So how fast or slow the game rendered was purely down to the ingenuity of the developer.

I will always remember the Speccy with fond memories and my only regret is not switching to it earlier.

Critical Mass, the loading screen to the left and below, the game itself.

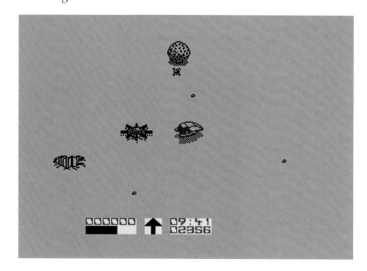

Ste Pickford

Ste partnered up with brother John to create many classic games on the ZX Spectrum that are fondly remembered, many on a budget label accompanied by an amazing 128K tune.

I made my very first computer graphics on the Spectrum, an act which, I suppose, led to a thirty-year career as a video game artist.

As a kid I always wanted to draw comics, and would spend hours and hours in my early teens sat with a drawing board on my knees, making my own comic strips. My brother John got a ZX81 for Christmas when I was eleven, and I played games on that when he wasn't programming it. He got a Spectrum a year or so later. I played a bit on that too and even wrote my own little games, but I still spent most of my time drawing on paper.

John wrote a little graphics editor on the Spectrum, and I think that really captured my interest. It was a full screen

180, published by M.A.D in 1986.

pixel editor but it had no zoom or anything - just a cursor and plot / unplot. We had a 14" portable TV so I had to really squint to see the individual pixels and spent hours with that, drawing my own 'loading screens' for games we couldn't afford to buy.

I'd look through the pages of C&VG and pick the adverts for brilliant looking Spectrum games and then draw a loading screen based on the impossibly good cover artwork from the advert, learning all the tricks of avoiding attribute clash and squeezing A4 portrait designs onto a 256 x 192 pixel landscape screen. It was great fun, and a technical challenge, but not something I wanted to spend my life doing.

A couple of years later I got the chance to have a week off school doing 'work experience' at Binary Design, the development studio where my brother now worked writing Spectrum games like *Death Wake* and *Max Headroom*. I jumped at the chance - a whole week off school! I expected to be making cups of tea all day for the programmers but instead they sat me down in front of an Amstrad CPC 464 and asked me to draw a loading screen for a game called

Glass that was almost finished. Maybe it was just to keep me busy and out of everyone's way - I did the screen and they were really happy with it and it was actually used in the game. Then they asked me if I could do another - at the end of the week they asked if I could phone up my school and stay for another week as they had some more loading screens to do.

I was hooked.

At the end of my work experience, I was told there was a job waiting for me when I finished my O Levels in a few months time.

My vague plan after high school was to go to art college and become a comic artist but I'd been bitten by the game development bug and wanted more. I decided to temporarily put art college on hold and in the summer of 1986, one week after finishing high school, I started work at Binary Design as a video game graphic artist. The 'year off' turned into the rest of my life and I've been making games ever since, with comics being relegated to my spare time hobby.

On my first day at work I got started on a darts game being made for Mastertronic that eventually bacame *180*.

We came up with the idea of a floating hand aiming the dart as we thought that was more interesting than the rotating cursors all the existing darts games at the time used. My brother (again) had written a really nice 'windowed' sprite editor on the Spectrum. We'd never actually seen a windows-based operating system before, he'd just read about them

TIME 00:02:43 BOMBS:9 ENERGY:59%

in a magazine and programmed what he thought a windows OS would be like on the Spectrum for his sprite editor. It was a brilliant editor with variable zoom and full control of animation (backwards and forwards!), and using that I drew my own right hand as the animated hand in *180*. My first proper week's work, and I'm still proud of it today.

Of all the 8-bit machines, the Spectrum was my favourite to work on. It had the best tools (my brother's sprite editor, and *Melbourne Draw* and others for full screen work) and its keyboard was the best for controlling a cursor for hours (drawing with a joystick on the C64 was hell) and the challenge of overcoming attribute clash was always interesting. It's just a shame we didn't have any reliable storage methods as all my Microdrive cartridges from back then are long since unreadable.

I never did get to go to art college but I've never really stopped drawing comic strips, when I can find the time between video game graphics.

Flying through the sky in *Glider Rider*, published by Quicksilva in 1986.

Clive Townsend

Saboteur and its sequel were huge commercial successes for Durell Software. There were plans for a third title in the series that was never released. Maybe now is the time...

I first discovered computers in 1981 when a school-friend, Steven Hodge, bought a ZX81. Between us we learned to program through trial-and-error by typing in listings from magazines. The listings almost always had mistakes in them which presented us with a fun challenge in finding the bugs and fixing them.

There were rumours of a ZX82 coming out the next year (Sinclair had always been very unimaginative with their computer names – the ZX80 came out in 1980, etc.) so I signed up to buy one. As it was their first colour computer it was soon renamed to the ZX Spectrum and I started writing games on it in BASIC as soon as it got delivered.

Once I had a few games of sellable

Clive playing *Saboteur* at the recent Revival event - August 2014.

quality I approached a local shop in Taunton and asked if they would sell them. They said they would but said there was already a games company in Taunton and that I should speak to them first. So I visited Durell (named after the boss, Robert James Durell White) who liked the games and my graphical style but said I should really learn assembler to improve the speed. I hung around the Durell office all summer and when I finshed school they offered me a job. I decided to go to college first, but after a year I realised the job offer was too good to refuse and started work at Durell full time. Even though I'd left college, many of my friends were still there. So occasionally I'd sneak in and pretend that I was still attending. One of the computer science teachers caught me out, but instead of complaining he actually left his teaching job and came to work for Durell. He ended up writing *Thanatos* on the C64!

The first game I was asked to write at Durell was called *Death Pit*. I was still learning assembly language as I wrote it – so it wasn't brilliant. I was also working on a pet project at home with a Ninja as the lead character. It was a side-scrolling platformer but I couldn't get the backgrounds to scroll fast enough. Rob White suggested I make it into a flip-screen game which solved the speed problem. I then designed the games story, map, and graphics in parallel. There were no art packages in those days, so all the original art was designed on paper. I then converted the pattern of dots into binary and typed it into the source code. That pet project became the game, *Saboteur*.

The original code was written on an actual Spectrum. In memory I had the source code, assembler and object code. I'd work on a routine, compile it and then save it to tape. To test it I'd reset the Spectrum and load that bit of code in along with the other code, graphics, and data. After testing I'd reset again and load my source code and the assembler – still all from tape. It was a nightmare process.

My initial plan for *Saboteur 2* was to send the same Ninja out on another mission, but with a much bigger map. As I planned the game I printed each room on paper and stuck it on my wall. As development progressed, I decided to change the lead character to a female – a

risky choice in those days, this was years before *Tomb Raider* made female leads successful.

Fans often ask if Saboteur III will ever get made. This is a game I have wanted to make for a very long time, but before I can, I need to re-launch the franchise to the current generation of gamers. After much research and planning, Steve Iles, who is my producing partner, and I made an announcement at the beginning of 2014 that a new game in the series is on its way. The response we received was amazing; I was humbled by the positive messages of support after all this time.

A complete port of the original Saboteur to mobile platforms, made from the actual Spectrum source code, is in the works (so if you know any game play tricks from the Spectrum version you'll be able to use them) with updated hi-res graphics as well as the original Spectrum art and a load of new features. Keep your Ninja senses on high alert and watch out for more news on this.

Saboteur 2, where the player takes the role of a female Ninja - published by Durell in 1987.

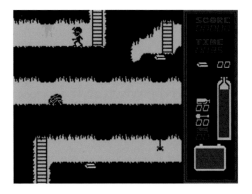

Death Pit, the first game to be developed for Durell by Clive.

Rich Stevenson

Short's Fuse was the first of many titles that Rich programmed on the ZX Spectrum. He moved onto the *Actua* series of games at Gremlin Graphics and gives credit to the Spectrum for his break into the games industry.

I started out coding on the Spectrum back in 1983 having already delved into programming mainly text adventures on its predecessor the ZX81.

Like many of the Spectrum coders of the day I worked tirelessly to endeavor to create the perfect game and I was lucky enough to be able to make a living from games development for many years. My reluctance to move away from the Spectrum would prove to hinder me in later years while other programmers moved swiftly onto the 16-bit machines and then consoles which had now begun to take over the market.

Like many of the 'bedroom' coders of the day, my early experiences of coding would be to exchange ideas and knowledge with school friends and other enthusiasts.

Short's Fuse, published by Firebird in 1985.

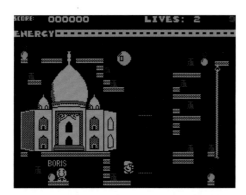

A typical Saturday afternoon would include a visit to the arcades before a stroll to Sheffield's Just Micro - a meeting point for local gamers and budding demo coders. The shop was bustling and groups of teenagers would congregate around the various machines located around the store, showing off their half finished demos which had been worked on throughout the week.

Interspersed within the groups of 'demo' coders would be established games developers who regularly visited Just Micro, not only to show off their latest games, but for inspiration when searching for that something special which would make their game stand out from the others. Tony Crowther became a regular visitor, and he would be a major influence on both myself and my closest friend Phil Durbidge, inspiring us to pursue our interest in game programming.

Our approach was to focus on taking our ideas from concepts to playable working games and ignore the urge to shelve our ideas whenever we hit a brick wall. Rather than showing our work in progress to the audience at Just Micro, we would ask for the opinion of my father who showed interest in what we had created, and supported us whereever he could. My father suggested that he could demo our games to a wider audience by taking copies to the various shops, which had begun to spring up locally. Armed with handfuls of duplicated cassettes, he would spend his afternoons visiting shops, insisting that the owners loaded up our games and would then show our work to anyone visiting.

An unexpected phone call during Christmas 1984 would give us the biggest break every bedroom coder could dream of, and led to *Short's Fuse* being published on the Firebird label.

Telecomsoft had been founded on the growing popularity of the computer games market and the formation of Firebird and their Silverbird label would give them a platform to entice young spenders to invest their pocket money in good quality, low-priced games rather than records and comics.

Their approach was to advertise for game submissions as well as asking regional agents to search for independent titles which could feature within the Silverbird catalogue.

Short's Fuse fitted their requirements well and became one of the showcase titles of the Silverbird catalogue and double-page advertisements.

The months of hard work played havoc on my school work and although we had become mini celebs within the computer department at our school, disastrous results

in my exams meant I would have to stay in education for another year. While *Short's Fuse* modestly charted at number 14, local software house Alligata approached me as they were looking to recruit coders to work in-house.

Alligata had already established themselves as a major force in the games market, publishing a number of very successful Commodore and BBC products, but the departure of programmer Tony Crowther to newly formed Gremlin Graphics meant a fresh new approach was required.

After toying with the idea of further education or a career in the games industry, I chose the latter and this would be the start of my journey into the real world of Spectrum programming. I went on to work on titles such as *Pub Games*, which gave me my first number one, as well as Spectrum conversions of Tony Crowther's *Loco* and *Trap* before the lure of a more creative role at Alternative Software was enough for me to move on.

Pub Games, published by Alligata in 1986 - a title that went to number one in the charts.

Mark Jones

Mark created some iconic loading screens and in-game graphics at the illustrious Ocean Software. Here he talks about receiving the Spectrum for his birthday and how he started using it to produce art.

Northants Computer Centre where Mark worked whilst applying to software houses for work.

Northants Computer Centre where Mark worked whilst applying to software houses for work.

Before home computers my weekends consisted of going up to my cousin Hayden's house who lived a short bus ride away from me in Northampton. We would go out on bike rides, hang around Weston Favell Shopping centre to make a nuisance of ourselves and go and look at Beatles' 7" records, writing pads, pencil cases and multi-coloured erasers. In the summer we would go to Billing Aquadrome, an outdoor swimming pool surrounded by holiday caravans. It was here I first encountered arcade games. I didn't spend any money on them, I didn't have enough, but I did watch Hayden and his older brother Paul playing on them. I remember seeing *Boothill*, which by 1982, was ancient even in those early days, *Carnival, Mr.*

Do and *Space Invaders* - mix the bleeps, squawks and tunes of those games with the smell of candy floss, hot doughnuts and pockets of Black Jacks and Fruit Salads and you can get an idea of the overall atmosphere.

Hayden, at some point, got himself a ZX81. I only took a passing interest in it as the black and white blocky graphics and lack of sound wasn't enough for me though I did enjoy having goes on New Generation's *3D Monster Maze* and Bug-Byte's *Mazogs*. This gave us something else to do on wet Saturday afternoons. I remember once that my go on *Mazogs* was up and Hayden turned the TV off and I thought that the game had gone and would have to be reloaded. It was much to my relief when he turned the TV back on and it was still there.

I was at Upper school by 1983 and my friends were increasingly talking about games and the computers their parents had got them. I had friends with Commodore 64s, VIC 20s, Dragon 32s and ZX Spectrums. Hayden had also upgraded to a Spectrum. Now, with colour graphics and sound my interest was starting to pique. I must have subconsciously been doing some research as I went to various mates' houses to check out a VIC 20, a Dragon 32 and Neil Anderson's ZX Spectrum. I remember playing *Bruce Lee*, *Jet Set Willy*, *Atic Atac* and *Jetpac* at Neil's. My mind was made up and I started to badger my mum and dad to get me my own Spectrum. A few days before my 14th birthday on June 12th 1984 I came back from school and mum told me to take a look between the sofa and the armchair; and there was a brand new ZX Spectrum 48K.

On my actual birthday I went to 'Northants Computer Centre' and bought my first games. *Trashman* by New Generation was my first choice, a wise purchase indeed. My second game was *Mrs Mopp* by Computasolve. No idea why I bought this, maybe I liked the cartoony cover. Got it home but I didn't like it, so tried to return in the next day with the old tale of 'I got two of these for my birthday' - but Ken at Northants was having none of it, so I had to keep it. Most of my school mates had Speccies too, so I quickly amassed a huge collection of C60s and C90s full of games. It was a great

time to have a Spectrum, we witnessed lots of firsts and groundbreaking games. I remember seeing the preview in Crash magazine for Gargoyle Games' *Tir Na Nog*. They described it as 'liquid animation' and it being a 'computer movie'. It looked amazing. Other milestones included the release of Hewson's *Legend of Avalon*, I spent many nights after school exploring that land. Seeing *Mugsy* running for the first time one dinner time when I'd gone home for lunch and, because the graphics were so amazing, leaving it on for the whole afternoon so that I didn't have to wait for it load once I'd returned after school had finished.

The ultimate (ha!) for me though was running to my friend Adrian Singh's house one freezing Thursday night late in 1984 as he had just rung me to say that he had the originals of *Knight Lore* and *Underwurlde* at his house for a few hours and (if I could make it there) was welcome to come down and get myself copies.

Mark (right) & his cousin Hayden around 1982 between dodging the monsters of *Mazogs* & the T Rex's of *3D Monster Maze*.

The receipt, inlay and tape for Mark's first ever Spectrum game - *Trashman*.

Early artwork produced by Mark on the Spectrum.

in to crude animations, which then (once I'd purchased *Wham! The Music Box!*) had added musical accompaniments.

Once my confidence had grown, my efforts were shown to my colleagues at my Saturday job in the computer shop. Their encouragement resulted in me sending off my work to various software houses at the end of 1986.

Even after the boom was over and I'd left my job at Ocean Software, I didn't put my Spectrum away. I worked at a different computer shop after that and cherry picked all the Spectrum software that was coming in, as people were part exchanging their 8-bit machines for Atari STs and Amigas.

I was retro gaming in 1990! I owned both 16-bit machines but, as is evident in a video taken at the time, I still had a rubber keyed 48K set up underneath those new machines along with an Interface 1 and Microdrive for when I was feeling nostalgic.

They'd been released only four days before. It was so cold but I had ran so fast I was sweating like a sow once I arrived. Seeing them loaded up for the first time was like nothing else that had gone before.

Break times, lunch times and after school was spent talking, copying, reading about and playing Spectrum games. I bought originals when I could but you're limited when you only earn £3.50 a week through your paper round. The situation did improve once I'd gained employment at the Co-Op and earned a whopping £10 for my eight hours a week there so I was able to buy my own games. These included *Stainless Steel*, *Sky Fox*, *Roland's Rat Race*, *Cyberun* and *Pentagram*. I was also able to save up and purchase *The Artist II* and *Art Studio* to help me with my experiments in ZX Spectrum graphics and practised a lot making on-screen graphics which turned

Concentrating on playing the latest game in 1984.

John Gibson

With solo projects such as *Zzoom* under his belt, John then went on to form Denton Designs, the team responsible for such classics as *Frankie Goes To Hollywood* and *The Great Escape*.

The Spectrum means a lot to me because it was the first computer I programmed professionally. I didn't choose to write for the Spectrum; the choice was made for me by my first employer, Imagine Software.

With the benefit of hindsight, I would still choose it over the C64 (the only real alternative) because I prefered to program the Z80 processor rather than the 6502.

The Spectrum was a very simple computer compared to today's offerings and that meant an individual could write games for it; a big was team required. This gave one a greater sense of achievement when a game was a success. For example, when Popular Computer Weekly gave *Zzoom* a review score of 100%, I could say, 'I did that', rather than, 'I did a bit of that'.

I spent the best and most rewarding years of my career programming the Spectrum and all my 'famous' games were on it: *Zzoom, Stonkers, Gift From The Gods, Frankie Goes To Hollywood*.

Games development was a lot more fun back in the Spectrum days; people were willing to die for their art, so to speak. It wasn't just a job, it was a way of life.

I'll be leaving the games industry when I retire next year and when I look back at those 32 years, it'll be the first few years that I'll reminisce about the most.

Above: *Frankie Goes to Hollywood*, published by Ocean Software in 1985.

Left - *Stonkers*, published by Imagine Software in 1983.

Fergus McGovern

By the age of 18, Fergus had started Probe Software, and with the help of Mastertronic as a publisher, developed a hugley succesful company that produced nearly 50 games for the Spectrum.

Every kid loved video games, and having the opportunity to make games has changed my life. I was fortunate to enter the games industry from a completely different angle to most of the programmers and artists during the early 1980's.

My neighbours Peter and Pam Fisher, in a suburb in South London, had been transfixed by a new type of technology that had been designed by Steve Wozniak and Steve Jobs, the co-founders of Apple Inc. In 1975 Steve Wozniak decided to combine computer circuitry with a regular typewriter keyboard and a video screen and in doing so gave birth to the first Apple 1. Pete and Pam Computers, who later became known as P&P Micro Distributors were one of the first Apple distributors in the UK.

I was 15 years old and doing my O Levels at school. It was all the rage at the time to have a Saturday job and by chance I noticed an advert in a local newspaper shop for 'HELP URGENTLY NEEDED'. So I phoned the number and it turned out to be my neighbour a few doors away from where I lived. I made an appointment for an interview and within hours I was hired by Pete and Pam (who were based in a little 3-bedroom house in Streatham). Pam was from the United States and quickly established links with Apple and the supply of the early business software from the large US publishers, such as the spreadsheet software Visicalc. However, they also imported the early Apple games from the States to complement the business software.

So, apart from stapling software catalogues together, helping shift boxes around an extremely small 3-bedroom house and answering phones, I was now also the resident expert in all things to do with the newly imported Apple games. By the time I was 18, I had witnessed the remarkable growth of a company start-up that was now turning over millions of pounds and selling hundreds of thousands of Apple II computers. But games intrigued me, so still aged 18 years old, I started my own company called Probe Software with a friend who was making

Commodore 64 music software.

We decided to make our first game for the Commodore 64, as this was a popular computer in the UK and Apple was more focused on business customers. The first game we made was called *Escape from Alcatraz* and we tried to sell this in local shops in Croydon, Surrey as a games publisher.

But no one took us seriously and we barely got our money back.

So, we made another one and the same thing happened. We soon realised that we were very good at making the games and had only achieved moderate success with our third effort called the *Devil's Crown* for the Amstrad CPC.

At this time we had not really focused on the Spectrum. In fact, I could not really understand how the programmers could actually type on the rubber keyboard as I was used to the now popular Apple II and Commodore 64 keyboards. It was only after a chance meeting with a legend in the games industry, Mr Frank Herman, who was the owner of a hugely successful budget publisher, that Probe made its first Spectrum game. Frank encouraged us to convert *Devil's Crown* from the Amstrad CPC 464 to the Spectrum 48K but this time, Mastertronic would publish the title and not my fledgling company. This was a great relationship; we would design, program, and build the complete game with in-game art, music and sound effects and Mastertronic, for their part, would fund and publish our game.

And this was the birth of Probe, the games developer.

We were now making more and more games and the company grew very rapidly. We realised that there was lots of great development talent in the UK that had experienced the same problem as Probe, trading as a small publisher. We targeted only the best and Probe became one of the big hitters of the British games scene.

This attracted the titans of the day; US Gold, Ocean, Activision and Firebird who all wanted Probe to make their next big hit and Christmas number one. These companies were specializing in licenses from arcade coin ops owned by Capcom, Sega and Taito to Hollywood movie tie-ins; and Probe was the first choice developer to make this a digital reality on the Sinclair Spectrum.

Probe came up with a string of hits including *Out Run*, *Teenage Mutant Hero Turtles*, *Golden Axe*, *Sim City* and later transformed this Z80 powerhouse into one of the most successful console developers in the world.

With thanks to our Kickstarter backers whose generosity made this project happen.

Michael Ordidge
Chris Van Graas
Harlech Quinn
Tobias Hultman
Dom Robinson
Mike Parkes
Paul Weaver
Colin Anderton
Gary Phillips
Hurray Banana

Duncan Harvey
Sven Nilsson
James Persaud
Chris Redman
Andrew Wareing
Gareth Perch
James Shade
David Marsden
Andrew Kenny
Michael Jacobs

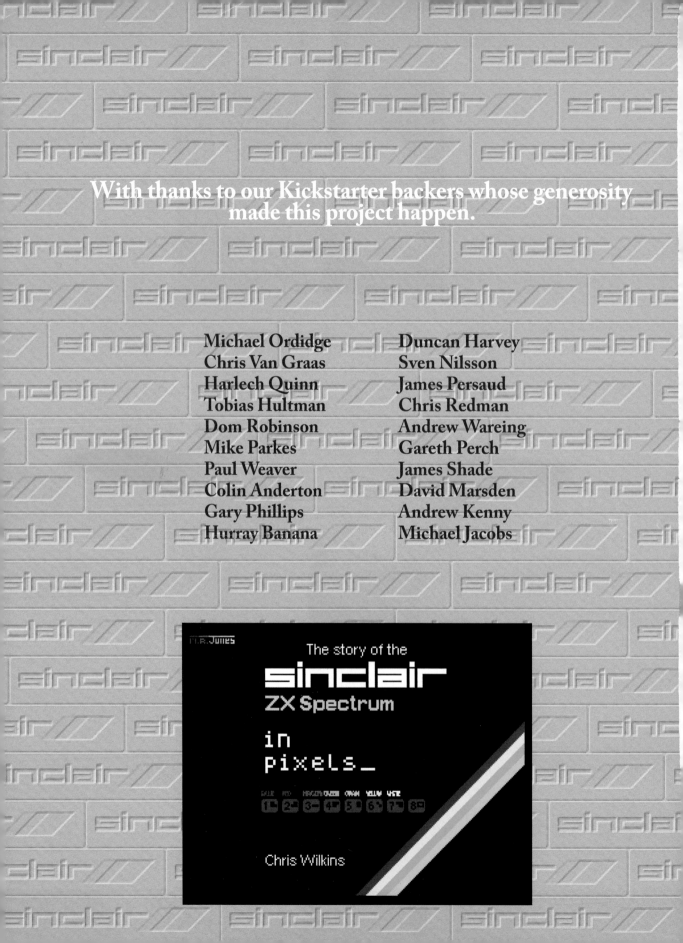

The story of the

sinclair
ZX Spectrum

in
pixels_

Chris Wilkins